The Beautiful Letdown

The Beautiful Letdown

An Addict's Theology of Addiction

David Tremaine

CASCADE *Books* • Eugene, Oregon

THE BEAUTIFUL LETDOWN
An Addict's Theology of Addiction

Copyright © 2019 David Tremaine. All rights reserved. Except for brief quotations in critical publications or reviews, no part of this book may be reproduced in any manner without prior written permission from the publisher. Write: Permissions, Wipf and Stock Publishers, 199 W. 8th Ave., Suite 3, Eugene, OR 97401.

Cascade Books
An Imprint of Wipf and Stock Publishers
199 W. 8th Ave., Suite 3
Eugene, OR 97401

www.wipfandstock.com

PAPERBACK ISBN: 978-1-5326-4615-7
HARDCOVER ISBN: 978-1-5326-4616-4
EBOOK ISBN: 978-1-5326-4617-1

Cataloguing-in-Publication data:

Names: Tremaine, David, author.

Title: The beautiful letdown : an addict's theology of addiction / David Tremaine.

Description: Eugene, OR: Cascade Books, 2019 | Includes bibliographical references.

Identifiers: ISBN 978-1-5326-4615-7 (paperback) | ISBN 978-1-5326-4616-4 (hardcover) | ISBN 978-1-5326-4617-1 (ebook)

Subjects: LCSH: Compulsive behavior—Religious aspects—Christianity | Recovery movement—Religious aspects—Christianity | Church work with recovering addicts | Habit breaking—Religious aspects—Christianity | Sex addiction

Classification: BV4598.7 T725 2019 (print) | BV4598.7 (ebook)

Manufactured in the U.S.A.   JULY 29, 2019

This book is dedicated to George and to Mary Lynn,
without whom it would not have come to be.

Table of Contents

Introduction

The Addict, The Bottom, The Invitation

It starts deep down in my stomach, in a place beyond the physical limits of my body, deeper than I can imagine any part of me can go. It is like a wave of warm water crashing through me as it slowly works its way up through my stomach and into my chest. I feel my heart start to race. It beats faster and faster and faster as the tide rises up past my heart, through my throat, and finally bursts forth into my mind like a tidal wave of excitement, fear, possibilities, desires, and needs. It stays there, engulfing my mind like a flood. The feeling grows stronger with every wave that crashes through me, in ever-intensifying currents, and comes from deeper and deeper down. As the waves pound against my brain the sound of the crashing turns into a powerful voice. It becomes louder and louder, making more and more sense, convincing me that whatever it is I am desiring, whatever it is that I am about to do, is worth it. No matter how much I don't want to do it, no matter how many people I will hurt, no matter how much it will hurt me, that relentless voice continues its argument.

In this moment, there is only one way to answer this deeply burning desire that has washed over me. There is only one thing that will satisfy this need. There is only one way to survive the flood. In this moment, the world shrinks. Like a drowning person struggling for the next gasp of air, my whole life is just this moment. The water closes in and it feels like there is nothing in the world except that next breath. The flood becomes my only reality, the sound of the waves the only voice of reason. Like a distant memory, I know that it is not the answer, but still I act. For a moment, or for many moments, or for hours at a time, it feels as if I have grasped the eternal, touched the transcendent, and gulped down that first breath of survival, of new life. It feels as though I have reached out my hand in one swift motion and finally grabbed all the peace, joy, and beauty that the world can offer. And then, without fail, it is all over.

Even faster than they came, the waters recede, and I realize my emptiness. As the waves move back into my depths I realize that my attempt has failed. When it is all over, when I have once again come crashing back down into reality, I know that I am powerless, that I have sinned, that I am, without a doubt, addicted. But inevitably the tide comes in again and I forget myself, and I forget the world, convinced that I can keep myself afloat, that I am in control, that I have all the answers, that my next breath is in my own hands.

My name is David and I am a recovering sex addict.

The Addict

I started looking at internet pornography when I was twelve years old and I walked into my first Sex Addicts Anonymous meeting when I was twenty-six. For fourteen years, from the moment I first searched the internet for pornography to the moment I admitted I was a sex addict, my addiction ruled my life. Half of my time I spent obsessing about what kind of pornography I was going to search for when I got home, the other half I spent scouring the internet for the perfect video or image. Like a constant drip of water changes the shape of a rock over time, pornography changed my brain. Every person, every relationship became an object for my consumption. I was bound, mind, body, and heart. I was in a prison of my own making, with walls fashioned out of guilt and shame, secrecy and deception, fear and anxiety. At the time I admitted that I had an addiction, it had spanned over half of my life. It started in middle school and lasted through high school. It was with me through college and into my second year of seminary, where I was in the process of becoming an Episcopal priest. It was with me through a committed high-school relationship, which turned into a committed college relationship, which turned into a four-year marriage. It was still with me when that marriage ended, no longer able to stay afloat amidst the flood of lying and deception.

I spent a lot of time over those fourteen years wondering what was wrong with me and asking myself why I couldn't stop. Every day I worried about getting caught. My addiction was my deepest, darkest secret. It made me feel broken, dirty, evil, lost, forgotten, frustrated, angry, and sad. While this particular addiction was not causing much physical harm to me or the people around me, it was consuming me from the inside. It was tying me up in knots. It was affecting my relationships, making them decay from the inside out. So much of my energy was either going toward acting out, covering up my acting out, or thinking about acting out. I was surviving, I was covering my tracks, I was building sturdy walls to keep people from getting close enough to find out about this part of me I hated so much. Every decision I made was about keeping it all hidden away. My only goal was to never get caught, to never be discovered. That, and acting out through watching pornography. This was my ultimate concern.

Amidst this frenzied chaos I was still convinced that I could keep it all together and lead the life I wanted to lead the way I wanted to lead it. I would be married, be a priest, be respected, be a moral standard, be loved and admired—and all the while be rotting away on the inside. As this way of life went on, these two sides of me became increasingly distant and polarized. The public side shone brighter and lighter, while the dark side became darker and more destructive. I believed that if I just worked hard enough, thought fast enough, and stayed one step ahead of everyone I could have both sides, forever. I lied to myself, convinced that I had figured everything out: myself, my spouse, God, religion, spirituality. I had my life and my world in a death grip, until it all crumbled to pieces in my hand, and the things I never wanted anyone to know about became the things that everyone knew. Humiliated and stripped of everything I thought I had, I landed in the place I told myself I would never be. This is what I had always thought would be the end of the world, the end of my life. And yet, I was still alive. This place, where everything falls apart and even the darkest crevices come to light, is affectionately known as rock bottom.

The Bottom

Rock bottom is a term coined by the addiction and recovery community to describe the feeling of having lost everything due to addiction. Often it describes a turning point where circumstances have reached their worst and the only options are to change or die. For most people it conjures up images of broken relationships, poor health, and dangerous circumstances. While it can be and often is all those things, it proves itself to be a much more finely textured and life-changing place than most expect before arriving there, though it is never a place to which one chooses to go. Anyone who recognizes having been there would likely tell you that they spent most of their lives trying to avoid it. It is a place of deep pain and desolation. It is also a place where everything has finally been stripped away and, lying face down in the ashes, we come face to face with the mysterious, unknowable, uncontrollable, chaotic depth of ourselves, "the depth of God."[1]

During my second year in seminary I fell in love with someone, someone who was not my wife, and I realized a depth of love that I had never felt before. That yearning for intimacy, which had caused so much suffering, led me to someone with whom I found this infinite depth of love, and am still in love with today. My eyes and my heart had been cracked open, and I could never go back to living the illusion that I had been living for so long. My marriage suffered a slow and painful death, ultimately ending in divorce, and I finally admitted to myself that I was a sex addict, addicted to pornography. The walls, the façade, the persona, the illusion of "morality," all came tumbling down, and I went down with it.

I woke up at rock bottom on August 30, 2014. I had just ended a marriage in which my actions over the previous nine years had led to distrust and emotional pain for me and my spouse. Following our separation, my bank account essentially depleted to zero, I took some time away from school and began a year doing an internship back in my home state, living in a town in which I had never lived and knew no one. Not only that, but the person I loved, the only person I wanted to be able to see, was hundreds of miles away and out of touch. I was broken and alone, living in a one-bedroom basement apartment. Literally, rock bottom.

It felt like everything was gone. All of my efforts to save myself had failed. Those walls of lies that I had built to prop myself up had come down. My delicately constructed defenses crumbled around me and as I fell with them, I felt that I may never land. It felt like I may fall forever. At the same time, that falling began to feel like being ever so softly, ever so gently, held. The falling was in itself a holding. The crumbling was itself a recreation. The death was itself life. When everything was gone—my image, my security, my certainty—the only thing left was the simple fact that I still existed. The object of my addiction, the thing I thought was the most important thing in the world, had let me down. It had dropped me into the bottomless depth of myself: a depth that I never would have known if it weren't for my fall, a fall that I never would have experienced without being addicted. My addiction was an invitation to something more, to something unfinished and yet

1. Catherine Keller, *Face of the Deep: A Theology of Becoming*, 231.

whole, to something eternal and always becoming, to something true and still developing. It was an invitation from God, one that I had carried with me for so long, but had never opened—until it opened me.

The Invitation

What if instead of thinking about addiction as a disease that needs treatment, an epidemic that needs eradication, or a moral failing that implies weakness, we saw it as a hand-written invitation from God? How would we operate differently if we saw addiction as an invitation to union with the transcendent, to knowledge of our true selves, and to spiritual depth and wholeness? How would we respond differently to those we know and love who are addicted? How would we treat ourselves differently in the face of our own addictions? Do you see how this way of thinking can change the way we understand and respond to our own suffering and the suffering of others?

Addiction is not something to hate, to run from, or to disown. We can no more label the experience of addiction a simple human tragedy than we can label the crucifixion one. There is something more to it than meets the eye. There is a "joy set before" us (Heb 12:2 NRSV), a promise present in this excruciating experience. In all its pain and fear it is something to grasp, to run toward. If we do, it will lead us to vibrant life, to our true selves, and to peace. Each one of us has received this hand-written invitation and now is our chance to examine how we will respond. It is an invitation that we do not discover in our happy times, in our religious devotion, or in our own moral purity. No, it is one that finds us through the very parts of ourselves that we wish didn't exist, that we tried with every ounce of energy to hide. If our addictions—our sins—are our invitation, how much longer can we afford to throw them away?

This is the question of our lives.

1

What Is an Addiction?

The first time I remember seeing pornography was in the basement of my friend's house when I was in sixth grade. It was 1999 and the internet was becoming a more normalized part of the average American life. Almost everyone I knew had a computer, and all my friends at school were chatting every night on AOL Instant Messenger. The vast complexity and endless resources of the internet were just beginning to dawn on me and my friends at that perfect early age of prepubescence.

I could find information for school projects without even stepping foot in the library. I could listen to music, communicate with friends, play games, and go to any website in the world. Anything I wanted to see or hear was right at my fingertips—and what I wanted most was sex. I wanted anything and everything about sex. Like generations of middle schoolers and prepubescent teens before me, I thought about sex all the time. I wanted to see pictures, movies, and TV shows, anything that came even close to risqué, provocative, or sexual. What was different about me, compared to all those generations before me, was that I was coming of age with the internet. I was not sneaking into R-rated movies. I wasn't stealing dirty magazines. I wasn't scrounging around the real world for sex—I didn't have to. It was all right there, free of charge, right at my fingertips, whenever I wanted it. Whenever I could be alone with the computer I could be alone with sex.

It all started with nude photos. It all started in that basement. Four of us gathered around a computer, one sitting at the keyboard, like the leader of a research team showing a group of fellow scientists an earth-shattering new discovery, showing us that there were websites with nude photos of women.

This particular website was devoted to WWF (now WWE) "Divas," or female wrestlers in the World Wrestling Federation entertainment industry. At the time we were all infatuated with professional wrestling, and especially these hypersexualized women we had seen displayed so provocatively on television and about whom we had often fantasized. Now they were right here in front of us, completely nude. That was all it took. I felt that thrill bubbling up from deep inside of me, tugging at my insides. I had struck gold.

From that day forward so much of my physical and mental energy went toward what I now in recovery call "sexual acting out." This includes compulsively masturbating, searching endlessly for pornography, obsessing for hours and days about women, watching and looking at pornography in all varieties of media. It all began in that basement with that wrenching feeling somewhere deep down in my stomach, far below the surface.

The feeling always started somewhere much deeper within myself than I could ever comprehend. It always ended with feelings of shame, fear, self-hatred, anger, inadequacy, and warped relationships, but I couldn't stop myself. It was the one thing that I always went back to and needed more than anything else. That ravenous yearning always came back, taking me over, possessing me, removing me from myself. I needed that pornography. For so many reasons I knew I needed it, went back to it, wanted more of it; and every time it let me down. It destroyed me more and more. Every time I thought it was the answer, and it never was.

A New Invitation

At first glance, addiction looks like something evil, destructive, deadly, and deceitful—and that's because it is. It destroys people's lives, bodies, and relationships. It warps interactions, rewires our brains, and manipulates the way we perceive the world around us. It is all these things, but it is so much more. In my life, I have felt these effects through my addiction. I have lied. I have devalued, manipulated, and obsessed about other people. I have been rewired, destroyed, and seen my relationships fall to pieces. Yet, I am more myself now for it than I ever could have been if it had never happened.

We often define good as something that contains no evil. We define life as that which contains no death. We define holy as containing nothing profane. As an addict, when I shine the light (or maybe the luminous darkness) of my own experience on them, I can't help but see that these glaring dualities no longer hold up. In the light of my experience, the line between good and evil is blurred, the barrier between life and death is more ambiguous, and the distinction between what is holy and what is profane becomes incoherent and unhelpful.

If we stop for a moment to examine the phenomenon of addiction, and gently take it apart without preconception or assumption, this uniquely human experience can teach us much about ourselves, one another, and God. It can reveal to us the deepest truths of our spiritual lives and journeys. It is a mistake to look for such revelation solely in historical dogmas and Scripture and ignore the wisdom of our human experience, because we are made "in the image of God"[1] (Gen 1:27), the ultimate and infinite mystery. Not only that, but the Christian tradition holds that this mystery became enfleshed in the life of a human person, Jesus of Nazareth. What more evidence do we need that our human experiences are themselves sources of revelation and that there is truth to be found in the living of our spiritual journey?

The human experience of addiction is a mystery, and our impulse in the face of mystery is to label, name, and diagnose. Today, we find ourselves in the midst of a growing number of people recognizing addictions to prescription or illegal opioids in the United States and around the world, a phenomenon now widely labelled as the "opioid epidemic." Understandably, this "epidemic" has caused a frenzy of fearful and anxious behavior on a nationwide and worldwide scale. In the face of these reactions, that which is hidden in this deeply spiritual human experience of addiction is overlooked. The mysterious, still, small voice of God, the mustard seed of the kingdom of heaven, and the pearl of great price get trampled on and buried deep under the layers of well-meaning attempts to destroy the cause of our suffering.

For too long Christian communities have let this vital experience pass through our doors without letting it influence our theology, our reading of Scripture, or our approaches to our own spirituality. As we peel back the layers of addiction we discover a deeper invitation beyond the labels, names, and diagnoses. What we call addiction is more than just physiological chemical dependence, and it is more than drugs and gambling. Addiction points beyond itself to something much deeper going on within humanity—not just some of humanity, but the whole human experience.

---

1. All Bible quotations are from the New Revised Standard Version unless otherwise stated.

Our constructs of addiction have led to the personal and cultural alienation and ostracization of those who identify as addicts. We now have an opportunity to understand it anew, as a vital part of our human experience, and to understand it as an invitation. On a larger cultural level, this is an invitation to reimagine Christian theology through the lens of human experience as it continues to develop and reveal itself to us. On a personal level, it is an invitation to each of us from God to depth, wholeness, and salvation.

As we reimagine a deeply ingrained concept such as "addiction," language is at the same time the most helpful and the most hindering tool. This book is about redefining and reimaging some of our most deeply ingrained assumptions. From the beginning, it is important to note that all language is limiting and in every case points to a much deeper mystery than any word can ever fully contain. While we are forever bound by the limitations of language, we are also set free by it if we are humble before its equally powerful limitations and possibilities.

What Is an Addiction?

In our modern vernacular, we use the word addiction in many different ways. We use it to describe things that we like or use a little too much, whether that is in a serious context, speaking about chemically altering substances, or in a more lighthearted sense, speaking about things like playing Candy Crush or binge-watching Netflix. As most understand it today, the word addiction is used to describe the experience of not being able to stop doing some sort of pleasure-seeking behavior. When you think of an addiction, or an addict, what are the images that come into your mind? What do you associate with addiction? If we survey the landscape of history, as well as our current rhetoric around addiction, the picture that we see is jumbled and disjointed. At various times throughout history, and in various cultural contexts today, addiction has been seen as a moral failure, a weakness of will, the inability to make healthy choices, a mental illness, a disease, a product of sinful human nature, or a hereditary dysfunction, just to name a few.

Over the last century the response to addiction has become very black and white. This is to be expected, as so often our reaction to things we don't understand is fearful, dualistic, and adversarial. Especially in the current climate of fear surrounding the increasing use of opioids, we have entire government agencies strategizing on how to destroy the epidemic, as hundreds of thousands, if not millions of people, are becoming addicted to prescription pain medication, heroin, and other opiates. This prompts us to view addiction as the ultimate enemy, the object of an unending fight for life and death. In the face of this kind of response we are not left with many options. Overall, addiction has become either a source of shame, an invasive disease that requires medical treatment to remove, or an enemy of our national wellbeing. In the face of what are ultimately well-intentioned reactions to the painful realities of addiction, people are still becoming addicted, still hurting themselves, and still hurting one another.

Currently, the most widely accepted way to understand addiction is as a disease, an epidemic, and therefore, as a medical issue, the best way to treat it is with medicine. Since the middle of the nineteenth century, scientific research has made clear that there are biological and physiological elements to every addiction. This includes the fact that different substances lead to varying degrees of chemical dependence in the human body, and thus lead to varying physical complications when approaching a point of detoxification. Every day there are research findings coming out about the physiological and biological causes and effects of addiction which lead to new and vital ways to help people recover physically.

In many cases lifesaving medicines are necessary for people to survive and to break their *chemical* dependence on the drugs themselves, but if recovery stops at the physical there is great spiritual opportunity missed. Responding to addiction is about more than finding a path to physical surviving. It is about discovering a path to spiritual thriving, to deeper and more meaningful life, to living within a framework that is not bound by substances, success, power, or any of the other things to which we get addicted. When we only view addiction as a physical disease among other diseases, we negate the spiritual journey that is inviting us to deeper connection with God, with one another, and with ourselves.

The longer we approach addiction as an enemy, as an invasive parasite in our humanity, or as a surgically removable tumor on our morality, the deeper the gulf will grow between us and God, one another, and our own identity as beloved. In reimagining our spiritual and theological understanding of addiction we have an opportunity to move forward on a new path, to move from surviving to thriving, from reacting to responding and, most importantly, from fearing our addictions to befriending them. This requires us to reexamine our current disease model of addiction, and place beside the physiological and biological understanding of addiction a spiritual one that is based in our inherent and unwavering connection to the divine.

A Spiritual Disease

One of the main catalysts for the modern disease concept of addiction was the description found in the original literature of Alcoholics Anonymous, even though AA "generally avoided the quasi-technical term 'disease', using in its stead a synonym such as 'malady.'"[2] The original uses of the terms malady, illness, and disease in the 1939 Alcoholics Anonymous "Big Book" were meant as metaphors to help alcoholics and other addicts explain the baffling experience of addiction. They were pointers to the feeling that there was some part of them that was operating against their own well-being and was somehow beyond their control. They weren't meant to be understood as an ailment tied solely to physiology. The intention was to separate the addiction from the addict enough to allow for some hope for treatment and recovery, and to help people recognize that they were more than just their addictive and destructive behaviors. The disease concept that emerged from AA was not meant to be an all-encompassing explanation of addiction, but rather a starting point for understanding a complex and overwhelming experience that might aid in the beginning stages of recovery.

Even before Bill Wilson, the founder of Alcoholics Anonymous, used this language in the "Big Book," doctors were investigating the physiological and biological causes of addiction. As chronicled in the "Big Book" itself, doctors in the first half of the twentieth century believed Alcoholism to be an allergy, in that some people were able to drink alcohol in moderation while others, who were allergic to it, could not help but drink it compulsively to excess.[3] There was also understood to be some sort of psychological and moral impairment operating alongside this allergy. Amid this culture, Wilson, after being a frequent visitor to the hospital for detox treatment after days-long binging episodes, experienced a revelation about his own addiction.

He began sharing his story with other alcoholics, recognized a power greater than himself, worked with others on their own sobriety, and began meeting regularly with other alcoholics while developing the twelve steps

2. Kurtz, *Not-God: A History of Alcoholics Anonymous*, 199.

3. Anonymous, *Alcoholics Anonymous*, xxviii.

through experiential trial and error. In response to the medical understanding that alcoholism and other addictions were some sort of physical impairment and having experienced many of his alcoholic brothers and sister recover without medical assistance but purely through a spiritual process, Wilson and the AA "Big Book" referred to alcoholism as a "an illness which only a spiritual experience will conquer."[4]

Addiction as a disease took on a much different meaning when it moved into the field of medical research in the second half of the twentieth century. In *The Disease Concept of Addiction*, researcher E. M. Jellinek concluded that "anomalous forms of the ingestion of narcotics and alcohol, such as drinking with loss of control and physical dependence, are caused by physiopathological processes and constitute diseases."[5] Writing in 1960, Jellinek drew his conclusions from data he collected by surveying thousands of members of Alcoholics Anonymous. While his methods have since been criticized, the impact his conclusions have had on the scientific community are undeniable, as the disease model continues to be used to this day by those in the fields of addiction research and treatment.

In July 2014, the National Institute on Drug Abuse (NIDA) defined addiction as a "chronic, relapsing brain disease that is characterized by compulsive drug seeking and use, despite harmful consequences" and is "considered a brain disease because drugs change the brain, they change its structure and how it works."[6] They go so far as to liken addiction to heart disease in that it has "serious harmful consequences, and [is] preventable and treatable, but if left untreated, can last a lifetime."[7] Jellinek had a similar understanding of addiction as a disease when he wrote, "it would appear that the acquisition of the 'disease' is in a limited way voluntary, but that once the disease form is reached it is no different from other diseases."[8]

The Danger of Stopping at Disease

While the Big Book uses the language of malady, illness, and spiritual disease to describe the experience of addiction, Bill Wilson makes clear that his recovery did not take place because of any medical treatment, but

4. Anonymous, *Alcoholics Anonymous*, 44.
5. Jellinek, *The Disease Concept of Alcoholism*, 40.
6. National Institute on Drug Abuse, "Drug Abuse and Addiction."
7. National Institute on Drug Abuse, "Drug Abuse and Addiction."
8. Jellinek, *The Disease Concept of Alcoholism*, 14.

rather through a spiritual experience. He says, "These were revolutionary and drastic proposals, but the moment I fully accepted them, the effect was electric. There was a sense of victory, followed by such a peace and serenity as I had never known. There was utter confidence. I felt lifted up, as though the great clean wind of a mountain top blew through and through. God comes to most men gradually, but His impact on me was sudden and profound."[9]

In Wilson's experience, a spiritual recovery was required for a spiritual disease. In AA's context, disease is used in its more general, rather than purely biological, sense. In the same way a physical disease causes a malfunction in the mechanics of a specific organ so that it is unable to reach its desired goal and purpose, it was meant to illustrate a spiritual dis-ease, a misdirection of something's intended function. Addiction, in this sense, was a dis-ease of the spiritual life, in that the spiritual self was slightly off from its proper orientation. There was something causing it to be oriented away from its normal alignment and function.

Shifting to an understanding of addiction as a spiritual disease was an important movement away from the shaming and blaming language that had dominated the cultural conversation around alcoholism for so long. Having experienced a spiritual recovery, Bill Wilson pushed back against the notion that addiction was simply a physical ailment, a moral failure or a weakness of will power. By separating the disease of addiction from the person experiencing it, he shifted the focus off the person suffering and onto the cause of the suffering. This was an important move toward a more compassionate and grace-filled view of addiction and opened the door for spiritual communities to provide support rather than judgment. However, over seventy-five years later, we have not moved much past this starting point to a deeper engagement with the addictive experience. We got stuck at tolerance, even going so far as acceptance, but so far we have missed the invitation to move into a new stage: transformation.

When we think of recovery as the removal of a wrong desire we assume that, like in physical health, the removal of suffering is the goal of a recovery process. This is the flaw in using the disease language of medicine to understand addiction. As with any metaphor, it has constructive contributions to our understanding, but it has significant drawbacks. Recovery from addiction is not about the removal of suffering, like a doctor might treat a dis-eased body with surgery or medicine to remove the cause of

9. Anonymous, *Alcoholics Anonymous*, 14.

the illness. Recovery is about the *transformation* of suffering. It is about recognizing that beneath what seems to be a human desire for evil is a deep yearning for the eternal.

When twelve-step groups or Christian communities use the language of disease this understanding does not get translated to the language about the spiritual. We end up simplifying our approach. Just as we can remove the "diseased" tissue from part of our physical body, a surgical procedure called "ablation," the goal of recovery from addiction becomes the removal of a diseased part of ourselves. This understanding has destructive effects on how we understand God, ourselves, and the world.

The scientific community has done and continues to do the important work of finding ways to help people survive and physically recover from their addictive behaviors and identify the physiological, genetic, and biological roots of addiction. As the witness of Bill Wilson and the twelve-step community have shown, though, addiction also has *spiritual* causes and effects. And while individual addictive behaviors may change from person to person and those physiologically predictive factors may change from person to person, the spiritual roots of addiction remain the same across the whole of creation. This is where we're missing the invitation. The scientific community continues to make strides in understanding and responding to addiction, but communities of faith are stuck in a disease model of addiction that greatly limits their ability to grow and respond.

By holding spiritual and scientific disease language for addiction side by side we can begin to see the disconnect that happens when a single term is shared by two distinctly different approaches to the same human experience. Following the linguistic path of the word "disease" we see that it began as a spiritual metaphor with AA, made its way into the scientific realm, and has now made its way back into the spiritual—only after taking on the characteristics of science. When communities of faith take on the language of science without checking the underlying assumptions of that language, they produce unintended theological implications.

In adopting the disease model of addiction from the scientific community Christians have taken the characteristics of a physical disease in the body and projected them onto the spiritual life of a person. This is not a one-to-one comparison, since we are taking the characteristics of something finite and applying them directly to something infinite. Addiction as a spiritual disease, illness, or malady is a metaphor. It is using the helpful language of the finite, the scientifically observable body, to help point toward *a* truth of the spiritual reality of addiction, but not *the* truth. We are left bound by this language, which was intended to be used as a helpful starting point for a deeper conversation about the spiritual implications of addiction.

Spiritual Growing Pains

The suffering of addiction, rather than a disease present in an unfortunate few, is like the physical growing pains through which we all suffer as our bodies develop. What if every person who suffered growing pains in their arms and legs when they were young was diagnosed with a degenerative joint disease? This would only lead to more suffering, unnecessary treatment, and confusion, as we searched for ways to end pain that is a necessary part of our physical journey. Rather than being some sort of genetic bone disease, growing pains represent a crucial step in our physical maturity, the universal human experience of the pain of growth. If we diagnosed growing pains as a disease and worked to remove it from our human experience we would be working against our own growth and resisting the natural development of our bodies. In the same way, the suffering of addiction is a vital and blessed part of our spiritual journey.

Like the aches in our growing bones, addiction is both painful and necessary. It is to the detriment of our own growth and transformation that we define addiction as a disease in need of treatment, rather than a vital and necessary part of our human experience. We must let ourselves be influenced by the witness of addiction, because addiction is not a spiritual disease.

Communities of faith may support "those people" who are addicted by offering meeting space, prayers, confession, and inclusion in the community, but even then, there is an "othering" that goes on. While a person may not be turned away for being an addict they are still understood to have a disease that can be treated, removed, and made better. This is where the disease language lets us down, where the disconnect happens between human experience and unexamined theology. Labeling someone as diseased, ill, or sick in this spiritual context is a distancing exercise. It may make us feel safe, it may allow for those addicted to feel accepted and included, but there is still a barrier erected when we say some have a disease and some don't. Inclusion and acceptance are important steps, but there is something more to which we are invited.

Beyond inclusion and acceptance is transformation, which can only happen in the face of mystery. Labeling addiction as a disease and stopping there is safe, but it leaves us separated from one another and closed off to the possibility of transformation through the mystery of addiction. Transformation comes in recognizing that there is a mystery in our midst and that there is a deeper truth revealing itself before us in the form of a spiritual journey. It is the realization that addiction is not a disease that some people have and some people don't. It is a spiritual invitation and journey playing out in each and every person. As psychologist Gerald May says, in reflecting on a long career of working with and researching addiction, "all people are addicts. . . . To be alive is to be addicted, and to be alive and addicted is to stand in need of grace."[10]

May's experience with addiction, both within others and within himself, brought him to the realization that addiction is a universal human experience that leads us all to "stand in need of grace."[11] But we can go one step further: *addiction is itself grace*. The root of addiction is not a malfunctioning part of an otherwise good person needing God's grace to correct it. The root of addiction is not a diseased spirit. The root of addiction is not our separation from God. To the contrary, the root of addiction is our *union* with God. The root of addiction is our *connection* to the divine. Addiction is not a deviation from what is supposed to be our otherwise good creation in the image of God. Addiction is from God. It is built into us from the beginning, as part of God's good creation.

If we believe that we can eradicate part of ourselves, all of which are created by God, then we are living in a delusion. There is no such thing as getting rid of parts of ourselves, there is only repression and hiding. The way we understand God, ourselves, and one another is at stake. I have heard fellow addicts talk about their disease as if it is their adversary, their greatest enemy. I have sat alone in many a darkened room after acting out and cursed the part of me that yearns to act out sexually in painful ways. Acknowledging that there is something you are doing that is causing pain is an important step in the process of healing and recovery. Naming it and talking about it openly are important steps that follow. But a surgical lopping-off of this part of ourselves or putting it into quarantine and throwing away the key cannot be one of the subsequent steps, because for as long as we think it is we delay our transformation.

10. May, *Addiction and Grace*, 19.
11. May, *Addiction and Grace*, 19.

From Abstinence to Recovery

One may think that the goal of recovery from addiction is putting an end to a specific behavior or set of behaviors like drinking, gambling, or sexual acting out. This is one step on the journey and part of the outcome of recovery, but it is not recovery itself. This would be referred to as abstinence, and there is an important difference between recovery and abstention. If addiction were just a bad part of a human that needed to be removed, then abstention would be the goal. This would put an end to the addictive behavior and keep the person identifying as an addict from further suffering because of that behavior. When the church prays for those addicted, we ask God to help the person stop partaking in a specific behavior. But recovering from addiction is about more than ending a behavior. It is an invitation to something deeper, to a recovery of something more essential in ourselves.

In the 1958 issue of AA's *The Grapevine*, AA co-founder Bill Wilson wrote an essay entitled "The Next Frontier: Emotional Sobriety." Though long sober, Wilson found himself in the midst of a deep depression that he could not seem to overcome. He worked the Steps tirelessly. He spoke with his sponsor and friends and corresponded regularly with other alcoholics dealing with similar depressions, but in spite of all his personal efforts, nothing seemed to change. Finally, after struggling for eleven years, he had a breakthrough in insight into his situation.

Wilson realized that even though he had gained so many years of sobriety, he was still crippled by even deeper emotional dependencies. He found himself relying on other people to provide him with the emotional responses he needed to feel happy and secure. When this ultimately failed to sustain his needs, he found himself deeply depressed, as the world around him consistently fell short of his expectations. The recognition of these dependencies led him to his conclusion that "emotional sobriety," the releasing of underlying dependencies on other people to fulfill emotional needs, was the next essential phase of sobriety for the alcoholic. Wilson described how this emotional sobriety led to a type of inner quiet far beyond any happiness, joy, or esteem he could ever get from outside of himself or his relationship with God.[12]

When we speak about recovery we rarely think about what that name implies. What, on the journey of recovery, are we trying to recover? As Wilson found in that first decade of his own sobriety, there was something

---

12. Fitzgerald, *The Soul of Sponsorship,*, 236–42.

more, something deeper, something beyond abstinence to which his recovery was inviting him. It is that "something more" that we will explore in the pages to come. Addiction is an invitation not to some sort of outward perfection, but to an interior integration of all the parts of ourselves, to reassemble all of the puzzle pieces that together make up the image of God in us. We are invited on a journey of recovering an essential part of our humanity; the connection to our own depths, the depth of God in us, and thus our union with the divine.

Until now Christianity has struggled as a faith tradition to respond constructively to addiction. Most of us are fine inviting twelve-step groups to use our basements and classrooms to meet during the church's off hours, but how do we engage actively in the process of recovery? How are we entering into communion with those who are hurting? How are we witnessing to the healing presence of God in our lives and in the lives of others? How are we invoking our theology and our tradition to witness to God's salvific work in humanity? Treating our addictions like a disease is not the healing response for which we so desperately yearn. If we step back from our fear and discomfort, from our impulse to explain away and control, we see a larger picture. We can see that all these experiences we call addictions are part of a grander narrative. All these parts of ourselves we would rather not exist are markers on the path of a greater journey than we could ever hope to fully explain or fully control, but one on which we are all invited to walk.

2

Spiritual Wholeness

What had I tapped into? There were no lengths to which I would not go to fill my desire, to respond to the irresistible force that was tugging on my insides. By the time I was twelve years old I had expanded my search for pornography beyond the internet to movies, television, magazines, and anywhere else I could find it. I was always on the lookout. It may have started with nude images on a friend's computer, but soon that wasn't enough. By high school I was scouring the internet for hours on file sharing applications searching for videos, obsessively watching the progress bar on my slow-speed internet connection. I did it every day after school, late at night, early in the morning, whenever I could be alone with the computer, the television, or any kind of media. It consumed most of my time and energy.

My acting out continued to feed my objectification of everything and everyone around me. I judged everyone as if I was auditioning them for a pornographic video, trying to figure out how worthy they were of my fantasizing and obsessing. Every relationship, every interaction, was to this end, and in that mindset, there is no relationship. There is no vulnerability, no intimacy, and no real connection.

My obsession moved from one girl to another as I was unable to focus on anything else, and finally I would return to the internet to focus this obsessive fantasizing on pornographic videos. Women, men, friends, acquaintances, strangers—everyone became an object for my consumption. I felt the pain of my addiction—the loneliness, the self-imposed cutting off of my friends and family, the secret that grew to overshadow my ability to be in relationship with anyone, including myself. It felt like a wedge slowly being driven into the

14

cracks of my life. The more infatuated I became with pornography the more everyone in my life became an object. The more I objectified the people in pornographic media the more I objectified people in my everyday life.

Every time I watched pornography, I immediately felt the acute explosion of shame in my stomach, the fear that I would be caught, and the agony of knowing I had sinned again. Beyond this acute sensation, each time I acted out I added another brick to the wall I was building between myself and everyone else in my life. I thought sexual attraction was the same as the yearning for relationship and connection, and that it was a worthwhile foundation on which to build relationship. I had stopped at this one dimension of connection and decided it was the only one. But it always led to more pain and more suffering.

The longer I lived like this the wider the gulf inside of me grew. I had a persona of a smart, competent, morally upright young man and at the same time carried with me this dark, hidden secret. The pornography-watching, secretive side of me became darker and darker, and more and more hidden. I became more and more removed from reality, from the pain of my actions, and from the ramifications of my acting out. The moral, smart, funny, personable side shone brighter, but at the expense of shoving this other part of me further and further into the darkness.

As the distance between my secret self and my outward self grew, so did the chasm between me and everyone around me. Watching pornography rewired my brain to see people only for their physical appearance, but that rewiring did not stay confined to only those people in the movies and videos I watched. It slowly spread to every interaction in my life. When I met someone new or interacted with people I already knew I could feel this gap between us. Slowly, subtly, I reinforced the bars of my own prison cell—one video, one picture, one fantasy at a time.

Made in God's Image

As Christians we are invited to view every human experience through the lens of the *imago Dei*, the biblical claim that humans have been made in the image of God. To be made in the image and likeness of God is to be made complete, sure that each and every part of us is "good" along with the whole of creation. These different parts of ourselves are "good," not in that they have the attributes of something "positive" as opposed to something "bad" or "negative," but "good" in that they are intentional. They are good in the same way that God, in the first creation story, looked at the different parts of creation after each day and said that they were *tov*, a word in Hebrew which is often translated "good" but also means "beautiful or agreeable."

All these parts of creation, all the parts of ourselves, are *tov*. They are exactly as God intended. There are no good or bad parts, there are only those parts which are *intended* by God and therefore make up the image of God in us. Addiction is not the deviation of one of these part of us which God intended for something else. It is as it was intended to be.

Parts of a Whole

The idea of having these different "parts" of ourselves is one that researcher Brené Brown uses in her research findings on shame, vulnerability, and human connection. Speaking at a conference in 2013, Brown describes this idea in more detail, saying "one of the things that I think happens . . . is there is an ideal of what you're supposed to be, and what a lot of us end up doing is we *orphan the parts of ourselves* that don't fit what that ideal is supposed to be."[1] Carl Jung, in his work on psychoanalysis, had similar theories of how our psyches develop over the course of our lives. Robert A. Johnson, a Jungian analyst, develops these ideas when he writes about what he calls our "shadow side" as "the dumping ground for all those characteristics of our personality that we disown."[2]

The shadow is a place inside of us where we put all of the parts of ourselves that we don't like or don't think are acceptable. Whether we use the language of "orphaning" from Brown or "disowning" from Johnson, the basic concept remains the same. From both the psychoanalytical perspective of Johnson and the sociocultural and interpersonal perspective of Brown, the evidence points to the journey of our early lives being one of paring down parts of our true selves and hiding them away to fit into the culture in which we are formed.

This is not necessarily a good or bad development. It is, rather, a necessary part of the human experience. It is a coping mechanism that we use to survive socially and culturally in the setting within which we develop. Our culture dictates to us from an early age which parts of ourselves are appropriate and acceptable and which ones are not. This fragmenting helps us as we grow to survive and be accepted, though it is only the first part of

1. Brown, "Why Your Critics Aren't the Ones Who Count" (YouTube video).
2. Johnson, *Owning Your Own Shadow*, ix–x.

the journey. If we stop there, then as we continue into adulthood, we begin to feel the pain of this fragmentation, and the yearning to return to the wholeness we know exists but with which we have lost contact.

The Source of the Search

Saying that we are invited to wholeness does not mean that we need to add pieces to ourselves that are not already there in order to become whole. What I and other authors, like Parker Palmer in his book *A Hidden Wholeness,* are talking about when we use the word "wholeness" is integration, or maybe re-integration. As Palmer writes, "wholeness does not mean perfection: it means embracing brokenness as an integral part of life."[3] One major part of our inner journey consists of taking steps toward reintegrating all the various parts of ourselves that have become splintered and broken apart.

Thomas Keating, a twentieth-century Christian mystic and Cistercian monk, writes extensively on his use of the spiritual disciplines of contemplation and centering prayer to do this work of integrating. Keating, in his book *The Human Condition: Contemplation and Transformation,* describes these practices as the most effective ways to get in touch with these various parts of ourselves. His assertion is that in the silent reflection of centering prayer, "when our defenses go down, up comes the dark side of the personality, the dynamics of the unconscious, and the immense emotional investment we have placed in false programs for happiness, along with the realization of how immersed we are in our particular cultural conditioning."[4]

What Keating is talking about here is a way to *engage* with our depths. In this example, the practice of contemplative prayer is a way to let go of our control over this chaotic depth of dynamics raging within us, allowing them to come to the surface. They are not meant to be grasped, forced into submission, or fought with, but observed, engaged with, and allowed to let their reality come to light in us. As he says, we become aware not only of the complex dynamics playing out within us but also the complex dynamics playing out around us in our cultural context and the way these inner and outer dynamics interact with one another, often without our knowledge. One of these dynamics which come up is what Keating calls our "false programs for happiness,"[5] which refers to anything we decide is going to make

3. Palmer, *A Hidden Wholeness,* 5.
4. Keating, *The Human Condition,* 34.
5. Keating, *The Human Condition,* 34.

everything okay in the midst of these chaotic dynamics. They are directly connected to this depth that is present in each and every one of us. They are our responses to those chaotic depths within us, in our struggle to control, numb, or overpower them.

Our addictions are our "false programs for happiness,"[6] but we do not call them false because they are wrong or evil. They are false because they are not the response to this depth for which we are yearning. They are finite actions when what we are *really* searching for in response to the infinite is the infinite itself. We are searching for a way to reengage with our depths and in so doing end up taking part in behaviors that we may believe are responses to the infinite but that actually cause us suffering. This transcendent, divine depth, though, is the source of the yearning. As Craig Nakken writes in his book *The Addictive Personality*,

> For human beings, pleasure opens up many important doors. It is the first door through which we can sense the Divine. Through pleasure, we can transcend our present state and step outside the limits of space and time. Sipping a cup of espresso, chewing a piece of perfectly cooked tenderloin, kissing a beloved, or watching a sunset—all these pleasure-centered activities can be transcendent. For a moment, we forget our checkbook balance, the crime rate, or a recent airline crash. Pleasurable experiences give us a small taste of timelessness. We can sense what it would be like to step into the eternal, to be held suspended in a worry-free, peaceful domain. But pleasure sensations, despite their transcendent quality, do not last.[7]

In Nakken's description of the addictive experience we can pick up this subtle but strong connection between addictive behavior and our connection to the divine. The "pleasure-centered behaviors" come from our yearning for the transcendent, timeless, and eternal, which means that we must in some way be connected to that very transcendence for which we yearn. How can we yearn for something of which we have no experience and to which we have no connection? These addictive behaviors are not destructive because of their intention or their source, but because they do not last. They are attempts at the eternal, the timeless, the transcendent, indicative of our inherent union with these qualities, but instead of hitting

6. Keating, *The Human Condition*, 34.
7. Nakken, *The Addictive Personality*, 70.

the mark of our actual union with God, we engage in behaviors that give us a taste of the real thing but prove themselves to be only fleeting imitations. Beyond the physical trauma that addiction can wreak on our bodies, this is the source of the spiritual pain and suffering of our addiction. It is so painful to feel this connection to God, to know it is there, to feel our connection to these eternal qualities, and yet, in our attempts to grasp them, to keep doing the things that hurt us instead. We know in our depths that the authentic experience of union with God is there, but we are unable, on our own, to find it. It is from this ocean of chaotic depth within us that our addictive behaviors emerge, and therefore they are not merely the source of our suffering, but *also* the source of our greatest potential.

Diving into the Deep

In her book *Face of the Deep*, process theologian Catherine Keller offers a theological reflection on the uncreated, chaotic, murky deep *(tehōm* in Hebrew) over which the Spirit of God hovers in the first chapter of the book of Genesis. She begins by challenging the orthodox view of a creation *ex nihilo,* the doctrine that God created everything from nothing, using this pre-existent *tehōm* as the evidence against it. She argues that from this *tehōm* God brings forth the rest of creation, and so the presence of this chaotic deep cannot be ignored.[8]

The implication is that this *tehōm,* this chaotic depth, is the source from which flow all the potentialities and possibilities of creation. Creation comes to be at the edge of this chaos: where impossibilities meet possibilities, the unknowable meets the knowable, and potentialities become realities. What Keller creates is a "tehomic theology"[9] of God working and creating at the edge of chaos. This chaos is not just part of a story in the beginning, as if it happened once and for all time and now is finished. This first creation story is happening all the time, in every one of us throughout our entire lives.[10]

The experience of addiction is one of great inner and outer chaos. It includes chaos in our relationships, in our bodies, in our brains, in our blood, and in our hearts. This destructive chaotic behavior, though, is indicative of our connection to our inner depth that is at the same time both

8. Keller, *Face of the Deep: A Theology of Becoming,* 307.

9. Keller, *Face of the Deep: A Theology of Becoming,* xviii.

10. Keller, *Face of the Deep: A Theology of Becoming,* 307.

the depth of God and the depth of ourselves. Our addictions are invitations to recover this simultaneous depth, sometimes referred to as our union with God, and to reengage with this chaos, this source of life and possibility in us. We are invited to engage with this struggle, to engage with the parts of ourselves that are darkest, that we are most afraid of, to re-engage and recover our connection to God-in-us, and dive headlong into the depth, chaos, and turmoil that is operating in us.

These "false programs for happiness,"[11] our addictions, are our attempts to take over this process and control the chaos rather than engaging with it and holding it gently. Instead of working with God in this depth and being held in this great process of integration and becoming whole, we try to take control and do all the work on our own. When we try to control the chaos, order the chaos, become God and take over the work of creation for ourselves, we feel the suffering of this chaos closed off from the hovering of God's Spirit over its face. In the midst of this chaos, though, lies a promise. The promise that when our attempts at control and order finally destroy us and bring us to our knees, and we instead engage with the chaos, that engagement creates the spacious "dome in the midst of the deep" (Gen 1:6 NRSV) within which the work of integration and the uncovering of our true selves can be done.

This work of integration is not a once-and-for-all end to a spiritual journey, but the lifelong process of integrating the various and continually emerging parts of ourselves. It is this process to which our addictions invite us; that voyage of recovering our connection to the depth in us over which the Spirit of God hovers. It is about our own ability to remain connected to this chaotic, unknowable, unorderable depth from which springs forth life, and to let ourselves be held gently to create the space for God to work with us in our own journey of becoming.

The Power of Powerlessness

Just as the chaos at the beginning of creation is the source of possibility, so is addiction, in all the chaos with which it moves in our lives, the source of our greatest potential. As Keller writes in her book *On The Mystery*, "the vulnerability of the flesh—whether to an unwanted temptation or to an agonizing death—cannot be wished away. But an honest embrace of our vulnerabilities may turn them into sources of empowerment. For those

11. Keating, *The Human Condition*, 34.

weaknesses seem to lie close to our strengths: our disorganization lies close to our creativity, for example, or our insensitivity close to our decisiveness. If the honest struggle with oneself that Paul recommends is engaged, the weakness that shames us can become a laboratory in a new kind of power. Our worst vulnerability can become, rather than the site of personal dissolution, the opening into an illimitable interactivity."[12] Addiction is a chaotic experience, a powerless experience, a vulnerable experience, but to turn toward that addiction, to hold it gently, to let it teach us, to befriend it, is to let it open us to the endless possibilities of ourselves. What we are recovering in the healing of addiction is the interplay with God, the "illimitable interactivity"[13] with God in us, in others, and in all of creation, that allows us to become who God is calling us to be.

There is a paradoxical truth in this understanding of our human nature, in that we are both created whole with everything we need already in us and at the same time on a lifelong journey of becoming who we are. As Keller says, we begin this journey "if the honest struggle with oneself . . . is engaged."[14] Thus, the first step of the twelve-step spiritual journey of recovery is to "admit that we are powerless" and that "our life has become unmanageable."[15] This is one of the great spiritual insights of the twelve steps, that the initial movement back toward our union with God and engagement with our inner chaos is a recognition of our own weakness, the weakness that can "become a laboratory for a new kind of power."[16]

The Shape of the Whole

There is a common phrase in religious, especially Christian, circles that we each have a God-shaped hole in us that can only be filled by God, by the transcendent. But how, if we were created in the image and likeness of God, could we have been created with any holes in us? As a part of creation made in the image and likeness of God, how can we be anything but inherently complete? We are invited to recover our completeness, the same completeness that we find in God. What, though, does it mean that God is complete? Jesus' words to his disciples in Matthew's Gospel about the completeness of

12. Keller, *On the Mystery*, 84.

13. Keller, *On the Mystery*, 84.

14. Keller, *On the Mystery*, 84.

15. *Twelve Steps and Twelve Traditions*, 21.

16. Keller, *On the Mystery*, 84.

God gives us one indication. In chapter 5, Jesus implored his disciples to "be perfect, therefore, as your heavenly father is perfect" (Matt 5:48).

This Greek word for perfect, *teleios*, includes the word *telos*, meaning end or completion, something having reached its final goal. It is not a kind of moralistic perfectionism. Jesus is not calling us to a faultless existence. This *teleios* is not about reaching a final goal of perfections, but about engaging in a *process of completion*, a journey *toward* wholeness. The perfection to which Jesus is inviting his disciples here is a process of *becoming* complete without ever actually *being* complete. It is this completion that Jesus tells his disciples and tells us that we share with God. It is indicative not of a final state of completeness at which we will someday arrive, but a shared journey with God of integrating all of our parts and diving into the depth of our inner life, the depth of God.

Our call to perfection is not a demand to be irreproachably ordered in our lives or stoic and static in the face of life's unfolding. It is an invitation to a journey that extends out one stage at a time, offering a more and more whole and focused picture of ourselves and God. In this way, saying that we all are on a journey of becoming whole is not like saying we are each a puzzle completely put together except for a missing piece or two, which we then have to spend our lives going out into the world to find. Instead, it is like we are a box with a complete puzzle inside, but none of the pieces have been put together. When we engage with our depths, with the chaos at work in us and around us, we are dumping out the pieces and letting them be put back together in us.

When the pieces are dumped out on the floor it is hard to decipher the image that the puzzle makes until you begin to put it together one piece at a time, just like it is difficult to recognize the image of God in us until we bring out into the open all the parts of ourselves that have been stuffed and stashed away in the deep dark corners of ourselves. At the same time, every moment of every day there are new pieces being added to the puzzle. This completeness, or perfection, to which Jesus calls us is a completeness that is, like God, infinitely unfinished, infinitely becoming, and yet infinitely complete in its infinite becoming.

Wholeness is a journey of becoming integrated with the infinite array of pieces being added to our puzzle each moment. We are whole and have all the pieces within us to integrate, and yet there are always new pieces to add to the puzzle. We are made in the image and likeness of God, in the shape of God. Jesus revealed to us that the shape of God is not a human form or a single part of creation, but a *life*. The shape of God is a journey that we walk throughout our lives, which Jesus modeled for us in his life and has been passed down to us in the form of the Gospels.

Therefore, it is not so much that there is a God-shaped hole in our being, but that the *whole of our being is God-shaped*. Our wholeness and our union with God are *one and the same*. We are already whole and complete. We already have everything we need inside of us, just as we already have complete and total union with God. We are on a journey to *re-cover* that wholeness by reintegrating those parts, a journey that starts with the realization of suffering, and a journey that we are invited by our addiction to begin to walk. This is our journey toward wholeness.

Strength Found in Weakness

In the behaviors of addiction, we are shooting for something eternal, and for something that our souls know is real and true. "We can sense what it would be like to step into the eternal, to be held suspended in a worry-free, peaceful domain."[17] Think for a moment about the experience of drinking alcohol. When alcohol enters our system we often feel an overwhelming, though temporary, sense of calm, warmth, and peace. This is alcohol affecting the chemicals in our brain and thus affecting our mood, and for a moment we enter into what feels like a peace.

It is as if we have found that peace that Jesus promises us in John's Gospel: "Peace I leave with you; my peace I give to you. I do not give to you as the world gives. Do not let your hearts be troubled, and do not let them be afraid" (John 14:27). This peace is real, but it is not found in a bottle, in a pill, or on a screen. It is peace as Jesus gives, but "not . . . as the world gives" (John 14:27). We yearn for this peace, timelessness, and worry-free state that is available, because our souls know the truth of it. In addictive behavior we are trying to get back in touch with this truth, this eternal quality, and, in our failed attempts, feeling the pain of missing. Alcohol, drugs, pornography, or any substance we overconsume in addiction brings the kind of peace that "the world gives" (John 14:27). They are not inherently bad, but they are finite and painful. In the midst of addictive behavior, we taste that transcendence and yet feel the pain of its aftermath, knowing it cannot be attained by the behaviors of addiction.

17. Nakken, *The Addictive Personality*, 70.

Addiction is the invitation to get in touch with our depth, the swirl of possibilities lapping constantly against the shores of our true selves, not rejecting it or hating it or labeling it good or evil, but just being curious about it. What is really going on in my addiction to alcohol, drugs, sex, or any other substance or behavior? What is it for which my soul is yearning? What is the transcendent quality of this experience that I shoot for over and over and over, and miss every time? When we see in broad daylight the failings of our addictions, that there is a depth from which they come and this same depth to which they are luring us to return, we recognize the invitation. We see that they are neither good nor bad, they just are. Because of this, our addictions are both our greatest weakness and our greatest source of strength. They are the thing that destroys us, but also the seat of our greatest power and potential. They are indicative of our yearning for the qualities of the transcendent, of God, but also indicative of our own capacities to miss the mark in our attempts at those qualities.

In reflection on my own experience of sex addiction, I realize that my acting out is an attempt at taking part in the deep intimacy, creative eros, and overwhelming beauty that is found in God. The way I tried to do that was to seek out sex, pornography, and nudity. All of this, though, was a shadow of the intimacy, eros, and beauty that I yearned for at the deepest part of me, and which always showed itself to fall short of the ultimacy that each of those qualities find only in God. Sexual acting out was my way of controlling what felt like an overwhelming, chaotic flood bubbling up in me, luring me back to the intimacy I desired, but in trying to take control of it myself all I could come up with was pornography. The pangs of desire, though, were from somewhere deep, life-giving, co-creative, and true.

The intimacy I found in pornography was under my control, but it was not real intimacy. It was fleeting and required nothing of myself, none of my own vulnerability or letting go. The beauty I found was under my control, but it was not real. Though it may have started with the beauty of another it was only ever objectification and created separation in relationship rather than connection. The creative eros I found was under my control, but it was not divine eros. It was fleeting erotica. Trying to control and order my chaotic depth led to death and destruction, but if I hadn't been destroyed by these experiences I never would have learned that I wasn't in control of my own chaos. I would have never known that I wasn't capable of realizing my own potential without the creative, loving force of God, and without letting go.

Addiction is our invitation to dive back into this *tehōm*, which weaves its way through our humanity and to which we are each connected. We are connected inherently in our humanity to God, hovering over the face of this chaos, inviting us back to it. God does not suppress chaos, order chaos, overpower chaos, but creates out of the chaos that is in each one of us, and invites us into partnership in this process of newness-making. In my journey of recovery, of reengaging with and holding gently my desires and of being open to how I am becoming, I can see that what once were my greatest sources of pain can become my greatest sources of healing and the seat of my potential and power. This is not the illusion of power that I was functioning with in acting out my addiction, but a new kind of power, a power whose source flows from inside out rather than outside in, from God inside rather than control outside. "The weakness that shame[d] [me] [has] become a laboratory in a new kind of power. [My] worst vulnerability [has] become, rather than the site of personal dissolution, the opening into an illimitable interactivity."[18] It has led me to "illimitable interactivity"[19] with myself, with God, and with all of creation, and folded me back into the flow of inter-relationship on which all of life is built.

Original Sin, Original Blessing

The opposite of the murky chaos we find in our depths is not order, it is stasis. This deep, oceanic abyss is constant movement, change, and transformation. It is awe-inducing in its possibilities, but it is also the reality of ourselves and everything around us. It is the truth of infinite change that moves underneath what we think is a finite unchanging creation, both around us and within us. Our addictions are indicative of our indifference to, or at least rejection of, the chaos churning in each of us, over which the Spirit of God moves to bring about our moment-to-moment transformations. Our true, whole, complete self is, with the rest of creation, always in a state of becoming, never actually having become. The first Genesis story clues us into our creation in the image of God as well as this eternal beginning, this creation from chaos that is always at work in us.

God is always yearning to birth newness from this chaos in us, but we have a role to play, and that is to re-engage our chaos, not try to control it, order it, or suppress it by playing God, but to let it be, and in so doing be

18. Keller, *On the Mystery*, 84.
19. Keller, *On the Mystery*, 84.

co-creators with God in our own lives. Everything that flows from this engagement with chaos has the potential to be positive, negative, or anything in between, but no matter what, it will always be *real*. It will flow from authentic relationship with the self, the world, and God. In this way, it will be good in the same way we spoke about creation in Genesis being good. It will be real, authentic, intended, and deep.

Each part of us that exists, everything that we are and that we have in us, is a part of this creation and makes up the image of God in us. We ignore the invitation of addiction at the cost of our own spiritual growth, wholeness, and potential. We demonize addiction, label it a disease, a deviation from health, to our own detriment. Our addictions call us back to engagement with the displaced, lost, and forgotten parts of ourselves, calling to us from the deep dark corners of our inner life.

Yet, before the goodness of our humanity can begin to sink in, we often can't help but find ourselves abruptly faced with the original sin of the second creation story in the second chapter of Genesis. The goodness we began with seems to have been marred forever, with the irruption of sin into our goodness, breaking apart our *imago dei* and leaving us deprived of the image with which we began. Before we can rest in the promise of this first creation story, the inherent goodness of our wholeness in process, and the invitation that addiction offers us as part of that image of God in us, let us examine the promise of the second creation story, the promise of the fall, the promise of sin.

3

What About Sin?

As I got older and my craving grew deeper, the breadth of pornography available on the internet continued to grow exponentially. When I went to college I had a new freedom, my own laptop, my own apartment, my own Internet. I was free to do whatever I wanted. By my senior year in college I watched pornography every day, multiple times a day. I found sites that were all free and available twenty-four hours a day, seven days a week. I could even watch it on my phone, untethered, wherever I wanted.

This only made the sexual acting out more frequent, intense, and risky. Not only was my drive for pornography limitless, the frequency at which I wanted to consume it and the intensity of the content for which I was looking seemed to be equally limitless. Like a vicious circle I kept needing more and more, pushing more and more, widening the gap inside. I continued to sort every part of myself into either the good side or the evil side, the right side or the wrong side.

It is hard looking back now to call any period of active addiction a time of freedom. While it seemed like freedom to be able to act out whenever I wanted, I was actually becoming more constrained in my heart, mind, and body. This is the vicious paradox of addiction. Freedom to act out was actually bondage. Every time I did it I slid another brick into the wall of my prison cell that I was building with my new "freedom." Every time I finished I would tell myself, "Never again. I will never do that again. That was the last time." Almost every day I told myself it was the last time. There were hundreds and hundreds of last times, hundreds and hundreds of bricks.

For fourteen years I feared getting caught. I obsessed about covering my tracks, erasing my search history, wiping clean the search bar, and clearing my phone. I lived in a world of religion, a Christian world, with two priests as parents and sex as something we just didn't talk about. It was never made clear that it was bad, but never made clear that it was good either. Sex just existed, in the hazy middle, looming. What I did know, deep down, was that watching pornography was wrong. I told myself that it was on the bad list of things to do. I knew that it was a sin, that I was sinning, and that I would be utterly destroyed if I ever got caught.

I don't remember any Sunday school lessons or Bible studies where sin was spoken about explicitly, but I knew, from the way it was spoken about around me, that sins were those things that put you at odds with God. They were actions that you took that were morally reprehensible and produced enmity between you and the Almighty God of creation. They were the nails that had pinned Jesus to the cross. They were things you did that hurt people without having directly done anything to them. They were the reason Jesus suffered and died. Simply put, they were bad things that God was angry at me for doing and for which I would eventually be punished. Not only that, but sins were actions that everyone else would be angry at me for doing too. I knew that this was what it meant to sin, and I knew that watching pornography was a sin too. I knew that if anybody ever found out, it would be the end of me, the end of people perceiving me as good, the end of people loving me, the end of my security, and the end of the world as I knew it.

Original Sin?

What is it in the Christian tradition that allows for the view of addiction as a disease? The disease model of addiction began with Bill Wilson as a first step in a larger journey of finding the grace that's in the midst of the addictive experience. Similarly, the current disease model of sin, finding its roots in the writings of fifth-century African theologian Augustine of Hippo, was the first step on a longer journey of finding God's grace moving in our experience of sin. As we saw in chapter 1 with addiction, we have remained stuck in this initial step rather than being able to move beyond it, to the detriment of our understanding of humanity, of one another, and of God.

In the early centuries of Christian history, it was common for theological writing to take place in the arena of opposition. Rather than setting out to write a stand-alone systematic theology, most theological figureheads of these early centuries spent their time and ink writing against theological positions with which they disagreed in attempts to protect the emerging orthodoxy of belief and smother any sort of heretical theological movements. Often, it is only these writings in opposition that have survived and so we are left to reconstruct the various heretical claims from the writings of the theologians that won the debate and whose viewpoints became included in the emerging orthodoxy. This is the case with Augustine's theological claims that ultimately led to the doctrine of original sin.

In the fifth century Augustine wrote four letters refuting specific theological claims of another contemporary theologian named Pelagius. As a proponent of asceticism and free will, Pelagius based his theology on the claim that the only divine act of grace necessary for salvation and personal perfection was the handing down of the law by God, which included the law given through the life and teaching of Jesus, and therefore humans have in themselves the ability to lead lives of perfection and good works without the continued presence of God's grace working in their lives.[1] Augustine responded with these various letters to push back against this view of human self-sufficiency apart from God and to emphasize the necessity of total reliance on God's grace working in each and every person.

One way he did this was to highlight the second creation story of Adam and Eve:

> In the beginning man's nature was created without any fault and without any sin; however, this human nature in which we are all born from Adam now requires a physician, because it is not healthy. Indeed, all the good qualities which it has in its organization, life, senses, and understanding, it possesses from the most high God, its creator and shaper. On the other hand, the defect which darkens and weakens all those natural goods, so that there is a need for illumination and healing, is not derived from its blameless maker but from that original sin that was committed through free will.[2]

Augustine's intention here is to highlight the glory and goodness of God's grace working in our lives and that it is only by this grace that we can do anything. In targeting what he saw as Pelagius' erroneous emphasis on the goodness of human free will and our ability to function apart from the continuous grace of God, he emphasizes two things very clearly. First, that

1. Augustine, *Four Anti-Pelagian Writings*, 8–9.
2. Augustine, *Four Anti-Pelagian Writings*, 24.

though our humanity was originally created without blemish, a condition Pelagius claims it still retains, it now "is not healthy" and has a defect that both "darkens and weakens" it.[3] His second point, building on the first, is that this defect came not because of any mistake by the "blameless maker," but rather entered into our humanity by way of that very same free will by which Pelagius claims humans are able to attain perfection.[4]

Augustine pinpoints the two pillars of Pelagius' theological anthropology—the goodness of humanity and of free will—and uses the second creation story of Adam and Eve to show not only that our humanity is unhealthy, but that it was through free will that it became infected with the darkness and weakness that made it so. In Augustine's view, we have no chance of perfection or of performing good works in the world apart from the grace of God working constantly in our lives. If our very humanity is compromised, and it was our free will that led it to be so, we cannot rely on either to bring about the love of God in the world.

Augustine's intention in these writings was to push back on these Pelagian views of humanity and free will, but not to demonize our humanity. His aim was to highlight the power and awe-inspiring beauty of God's grace working in our lives. He did not set out to tear down humanity's goodness or that of creation, but to raise up God's. In pushing back on Pelagius' claims of human self-sufficiency, though, Augustine created a narrative that highlights God's grace *at the expense of* the goodness of creation and paved the way for the disease model of sin that still permeates Christian orthodoxy and belief sixteen hundred years later.

A New Approach to Eden

Contrary to Augustine's reading, the story of Adam and Eve in the Garden of Eden does not claim that we were created without sin. The second chapter of Genesis says that "God formed [a human] from the dust of the ground . . . planted a Garden in Eden . . . made to grow every tree that is pleasant to the sight and . . . out of the ground the LORD God formed every animal of the field and every bird of the air" (Gen 2:7–19). If God created everything that exists with God's own hands, where is the space for a disease to creep into that creation? What are the gaps through which some sort of deviation can occur? The underlying assumption behind Augustine's

3. Augustine, *Four Anti-Pelagian Writings*, 24.

4. Augustine, *Four Anti-Pelagian Writings*, 24.

interpretation is that God's creation was never supposed to suffer or fall but to live in Eden forever.

There is another possibility, though, between the Augustinian claim that humanity brought the disease of sin into creation by deviating from the will of God and the Pelagian claim that we are without need of God's assistance in our spiritual journey. Through the cracks in the earth that accompany God in the beginning of the second creation narrative, a third way springs forth. One that does not deny the importance of God's grace working in our lives, but that also does not locate that grace solely in response to human failure.

This second narrative of creation, which tells the story of the interactions between God and God's many creations, has been the foundation for a disease model of sin for centuries. Augustine's interpretation of this story, and his theology of original sin, have made the space in Christian theology to assume the language of disease for addiction and led to our limited ability to respond to and understand it. As the narrative that undergirds this disease model, revisiting the story of Adam and Eve can open up to us a new way of understanding the place of both sin and addiction in our humanity.

This is a story of how we make attempts at the eternal, try to reach out and control the chaotic dynamics in and around us, and thus it is not just a story of sin, but a story of addiction. It tells the story of the infinite potential of relationship, the nature of our connection to God and creation, and the way that our addictions, our sins, call us back to deeper connection with God through the dynamic interplay of creation. In opening up a new theological space through this story, we may find that sin and addiction already occupy the same space and that a new way of understanding one can inform a new way of understanding the other.

Made from the Muck

Often, in our hurry to meet the first humans and dive into the intrigue of a serpent's deception, we skip over the subtle details of the beginning of creation as outlined in this second creation narrative. The author begins,

> In the day that the LORD God made the earth and the heavens, when no plant of the field was yet in the earth and no herb of the field had yet sprung up—for the LORD God had not caused it to rain upon the earth, and there was no one to till the ground; but

> *a stream would rise from the earth, and water the whole face of the*
> *ground*— then the LORD God formed [the human] from the dust
> of the ground, and breathed into its nostrils the breath of life; and
> the human became a living being. (Gen 2:4b–7 NRSV, modified)

In jumping to the first creature we miss the real protagonist in the story of Eden. We again skip over the chaos moving over the face of the text, or more properly, under it, and look past all that raw material in creation that precedes our human arrival.

Before there is anything else, the story of creation begins with earth, *'adāmah* in Hebrew, and a stream. This stream would bubble up from beneath the surface of the earth and, like the Spirit of God hovering "over the face of the [deep]" (Gen 1:2), it would water "the whole face of the ground (*'adāmah*)" (Gen 2:6). In the beginning, there was earth and water and they were both separated yet constantly recombining. The waters seeped up through the cracks of the dry earth and covered its face, soaked into the soil, and recombined to make the murky, muddy, water-infused earth from which God would fashion not only the first human, but every "animal of the field" and "bird of the air" (Gen 2:19). In the beginning of this second story, the deep, the *tehōm* of Genesis 1:2, makes its re-appearance.

The material that God fashioned into these first creatures, *'āphār* in Hebrew, is often translated as "dust," but in other places in the Hebrew scriptures translates as "loose earth" (Gen 26:15), "rubbish" (Neh 4:10), or even "plaster" (Lev 14:41). Would this anthropomorphized Creator God grab dry, dusty earth, to form these first creatures? If you were going to make something out of the dirt, would you pick the driest dirt you could find, or a wet clump of earth that can stick together, hold form, and be molded? This water that would spring up from the deep is the binding agent of our creation. It is what holds together the *'adāmah* and allows us to have form. We are not dry beings, we are mostly water, and when we return to the earth we turn back into this mucky muck from which we were formed. From muck we came, to muck we shall return.

Relationship Created

God took the *'āphār* from the *'adāmah*, the now-remixed earth and water from the surface of the ground, and formed every living creature. And why did God do this? "No plant of the field was yet in the earth and no herb of the field had yet sprung up—for the LORD God had not caused it to rain upon the earth, and there was no one to till the ground; but a stream would rise from the earth, and water the whole face of the ground—then the LORD God formed [a human]" (Gen 2:5–7). Though there was ground to cultivate and a spring rising up to water it, there was no one there to tend to the growth. The earth and water required a partner, a co-creator, to bring forth growth. Only after the human is created does God plant the garden in Eden, cause the trees and plants to come up from the ground, and a river to flow out of Eden, which becomes a multiplicity of waters, the four rivers flowing through creation.

From the relationship of earth and water God formed a counterpart for them, one to till the ground and cultivate it. Once God had a counterpart for earth and water, God realized that this counterpart needed a counterpart. As God had done to make the human, God fashioned from the ground and water more creatures of all shapes and sizes. Though they came from the same stuff that this human was from, they were not the counterpart the human required. So, God split this human in two to make another human. Often the story is told that God took a rib from the first human to make the second, rib being one translation of the Hebrew word tsēlāʻ, but the word more generally means "side." The implication in this word is that God splits this first human in half, and from each half fashions another human. What was once one human is now two, and thus relationship has been created between them. They are no longer completely enmeshed, they are now distinct, as is every creature that is part of creation.

From the mixture of earth and water came the human and all the animals. From the human came a woman and a man. From the muck, the ʻāphār, came distinct creatures, each one different from the other, and from difference came relationship. From relationship came all possibilities of creation, all the potential outcomes, all of which found their beginning in this murky, formless, remixing of the chaotic muck of creation. Thus, all living things—plants, trees, animals, and humans—were created by God. Every character in the story was created by God. There is no created thing—not the human, not any of the birds of the air or fish of the sea, nor animals of the ground—that was not each uniquely and personally created by the hand of God from this murky, chaotic formlessness.

Sympathy for the Serpent

In the next part of the story we meet one of the wild animals that had been formed by God from the *'āphār* with the human and the rest of the creatures. "Now the serpent was more crafty than any other wild animal that the LORD God had made" (Gen 3:1). No more an intruder into the Edenic setting of the story than the human, the serpent, like all the other wild animals, was made by God and was an intended part of this creation. Imagine for a moment that you've never heard the narrative in *Paradise Lost* in which the serpent was the fallen angel Lucifer in disguise, infiltrating the garden of Eden to bring about the fall of God's creation. Instead, focus on what the story actually says about the snake, the tree, the woman, and the man. Assume that, as one of the many creatures formed by God, the serpent was *supposed* to be there.

The serpent is, as God made it to be, crafty (3:1). This word, *'ārum* in Hebrew, can mean crafty, shrewd, sensible, prudent, or subtle. At various other places in the Hebrew scriptures it is used to describe both virtuous and treacherous actions of different characters. Even Jesus, in Matthew's Gospel, tells his disciples to be "*phronimos* as serpents" (Matt 10:16), which is the Greek version of this Hebrew word *'ārum*, meaning wise, shrewd, or prudent. Not only that, but this word is directly related to the word that describes the man and woman as being naked (*'ārōm*) in the preceding verse (2:25). The serpent is shrewd, subtle, and wise in the sense that it can make the truth *bare*, make *naked* the reality around it so that the truth can be seen for what it is. We have read treachery into the serpent's behaviors, but more because of the woman's passing of blame in the presence of God at the end of the story than because of its actions in and of themselves.

As a created thing, the serpent is free to move about the garden, to make decisions, and to interact with the other creatures. Here the snake is interacting with the woman. If we strip away our assumptions about the snake's motives, if we just read the story, what does it say? The serpent asks the woman to clarify what God had asked of them. "Did God say you shall not eat from any tree in the Garden?" (Gen 3:1). The woman responds, "not any tree, just the tree in the middle, nor shall we touch it, or we will die" (Gen 3:3). The wise and sensible serpent, the truth-barer, knew that this was not true, and told the woman that in fact she would not die. Rather, God knew that if they ate of the tree they would "be like God knowing good and evil" (Gen 3:5).

The snake didn't dispute that God said not to eat of the tree, the snake disputed that they would *die* if they ate it. The serpent didn't convince the woman that the rule didn't exist, but that the consequences of the rule were not what had been communicated. This is the difference between truth and trust. The serpent told the *truth* that *on that day* they would not die if they ate of the tree of the knowledge of good and evil, but that is not the same as *trusting* why God told them not to eat of it. The snake wanted truth to the detriment of trust. In this way the serpent is attempting to exert control over something transcendent, which is truth. Truth, though, is not something you can control nor is it something one person owns. As we will discuss further in chapter 5, there is no knowledge of truth outside of relationship, and relationship requires trust. This was not deception or manipulation, but an attempt at grasping and controlling transcendent truth, which led to mutual suffering.

The serpent believes that God made the rule not to keep them from dying, but to keep them from being like God, knowing good and evil. In the end, it seems like this may be a distinction without a difference, in that while they don't die the kind of death they thought God was talking about, they do experience a kind of death through this new way of knowing. They experience the death of the illusion of Eden. Their blindness to their own nakedness and to other realities of the world around them dies that day, the moment they eat of the fruit.

The snake knew the truth, but also could not believe that there was something more dynamic at play than that truth. There was a knowledge of the truth, but there was no trust in God that regardless of what was true, the rule had been set up for their own good, rather than for a selfish need by God to remain exclusively God-like. The woman, seeing the goodness, beauty, and wisdom available right in front of her, trusted the wise serpent and ate the fruit. Both characters were aiming at something eternal. For the serpent it was the truth about the world and sharing it with the woman. For the woman it was beauty, goodness, and wisdom. She eats of the fruit of the tree, and she gives some to the man and he eats, and consequently both of their eyes "were opened and they knew that they were naked" (Gen 3:7). The serpent, the shrewd truth-barer, made reality naked, and reveals to them the truth of their nakedness. Nothing in their humanity changes. It is their *perception* of reality, of what is already true, that changes. Through making the truth of reality naked in front of them, they recognize the reality of their own nakedness.

A Deeper Knowing

Immediately, the serpent, the woman, and the man feel the pain of their actions. They do not have to wait for God to punish them. Their actions are causing their punishment already. The story tells us that "the eyes of both were opened, and they knew that they were naked; and they sewed fig leaves together and made loincloths for themselves" (Gen 3:7). Here we have the first fruits of their actions, the consequence of obtaining the knowledge of good and evil. Eating the fruit didn't *bring about* good and evil, it didn't *create* chaos. Eating the fruit opened their eyes to the good and evil that was already there. It brought them to the recognition of how things actually were. It didn't change creation, it didn't make creation fall, it didn't infect it with a disease, it reconnected them to the chaos that was already and always there, to the potential for both good and bad, for both joy and suffering.

As we learned earlier in the story, the serpent was the most subtle and shrewd, and being able to see what was true, had the ability to make things bare. The first thing that happens after the fruit is eaten is that they realize their own bareness and in turn the naked truth of all of creation. They see that Eden isn't idyllic in that no pain can ever come to them, but instead that pain and joy are inextricably linked, that both good and bad can grow from the ground, that creation is a mix of every potentiality, not just those they might deem as good, but just what is.

Like the man and the woman, our eyes are opened through transgression, through addiction. The opening of the eyes of the man and woman to see reality as it was, to know themselves in a deeper way than they knew before, was not because of a magical fruit. The quality and content of the fruit were inconsequential. It was the act of transgressing this first law that led to their awakening and their knowing. It allowed them to perceive and be in relationship in a new way with creation and with God. It also led to pain and suffering, enmity and broken relationship, shame and fear, blame and uncertainty as the fallout from their actions becomes clear. They begin to blame one another, yet another consequence of their new knowledge. The man blames God for giving him the woman, completely forgetting that they are two halves of a whole, while the woman says that the serpent tricked her, when really all the serpent did was tell her the truth.

Restoration, Not Retribution

The story concludes with God handing out punishments, but if we take a closer look this list of punishments begins to look like the natural consequences of actions, rather than punitive measures passed down by an angry judicial authority. The consequences for their actions are all characteristic of the ways relationship has been broken amongst the different parts of creation. To the serpent, God says, "Because you have done this, cursed are you among all animals and among all wild creatures; upon your belly you shall go, and dust you shall eat all the days of your life. I will put enmity between you and the woman, and between your offspring and hers; he will strike your head and you will strike his heel" (Gen 3:14–15). Rather than being "more [subtle] than any other wild animal" (Gen 3:1), the serpent's actions have caused it to be "cursed . . . among all wild creatures" (Gen 3:14).

Initially, we read here the deceptive serpent being punished for its actions, forced by God to move about the world on its belly, eating the dust of the ground as it goes. Is this the nature of being cursed though? The story never says that the serpent walked on legs before the woman ate the fruit. The curse is not a change in the physical form of the serpent, the change is the relationship with the woman, and how that change will manifest in the different ways they move about creation. God did not add enmity to the relationship between the woman and the serpent, the cost of blaming and accusation on the woman's part causes the enmity in their relationship. God is not creating something that is not there, God is revealing the consequences of the woman's actions for the serpent's relationship with her. The serpent has been at the feet of the humans the whole time, but now the humans blame the serpent for all of their misfortune, and thus there is enmity, and that enmity will be transmitted to the children of the woman as the story of the serpent's perceived deception is passed down. Now, instead of moving together as equals in the landscape of creation, the humans will "strike [its] head" and in return it will "strike [their] heel" (Gen 3:15).

God moves on to the woman, saying "I will greatly increase your pangs in childbearing; in pain you shall bring forth children, yet your desire shall be for your husband, and he shall rule over you" (Gen 3:16). Again, is something new being added to the mix, or is this simply an already-existing reality being transformed in response to the ever-evolving relationships of creation? It appears that not only was there childbirth before the woman ate the fruit, but that there was also pain in childbirth. God does not say "I will make your childbirth painful," but says instead, "I will greatly *increase* your pangs in childbearing." Is this just the retributive justice of an angry God or is it the natural consequence from what has just taken place?

Imagine the woman's situation in Eden as the one tasked with bearing children. It seems that in Eden there were physical pains, the pangs of childbirth, but nonetheless these pangs were to bring a child into an idyllic setting, where everything is provided, where there is no danger, where there is no fear of other creatures and no enmity of which to speak. This is no longer the case, as the fallout continues. Enmity now exists between the serpent and the woman, an enmity that will be passed from generation to generation, so that there will be conflict between the humans and the animal, and the human will spend its days striking at its head and the serpent striking at their heel. The outlook of bringing children into a world of conflict, violence, fear, and suffering increases the pangs of childbirth. They are pangs of fear and anxiety knowing that a child is being born into a world that is not idyllic, where there will be enmity and suffering. This is not a punishment, but the suffering that naturally follows from sin and from trying to take control of the chaos of the world rather than engaging with it.

The chain of relationship has moved from serpent to woman and now it moves again from woman to man, as God says that the woman's "desire shall be for [her] husband, and he shall rule over [her]" (Gen 3:16). Again, do we find here a punishment handed down by a misogynistic, masculine, oppressive God, or is this the revelation of what will be true in relationship between man and woman as they prepare to be expelled from Eden? God, relationship itself, knows the relational consequences of operating in a world knowing both joy and suffering. God does not say, "I have set the man over you and have made it so that you will be subservient to him." Rather, God knows that in the world outside of Eden there will be abuses of power in relationship and oppression of the vulnerable, which are both consequences of fear and the perception of difference.

God moves then to the man, saying "Because you have listened to the voice of your wife, and have eaten of the tree about which I commanded you, 'You shall not eat of it,' cursed is the ground because of you; in toil you shall eat of it all the days of your life; thorns and thistles it shall bring forth for you; and you shall eat the plants of the field. By the sweat of your face you shall eat bread until you return to the ground, for out of it you were taken; you are dust, and to dust you shall return" (Gen 3:17–19). Here we move from the relationship between the man and the woman to the relationship between the man and the earth, the ground from which he was molded and created to cultivate. This is the completion of the circle of consequences set off by the eating of the fruit. The ground (*'adāmah*) will be cursed in that it will have the potential not only to bring about edible food, but also inedible. The man now will perceive the potential for both joyful and painful outcomes to be produced from creation, from his co-creation with the land. He was created in part to cultivate the ground from which he came, and he will still do this, but now it will be harder. There will be less certainty, an increase in potential outcomes, and he will feel every ounce of the work it will take to bring forth food from the land, the land from which he came and to which he shall return. Finally, the man is sent "to till the ground from which he was taken. God drove out the man; and at the east of the garden of Eden he placed the cherubim, and a sword flaming and turning to guard the way to the tree of life" (Gen 3:23–24).

Circle of Relationship

The life-cycle has been revealed, the inter-relationality of all things has been made clear, and creation continues its eternal journey of emerging. From the ground these creatures came to be, made from the muck of remixing the separated land and waters of the primordial deep. In their relationships with one another each feels the unique effects of transgression. The snake and the woman, once freely in conversation are now at odds. The man and the woman, not only having been previously equal but having previously been one in the same human, now recognize their physical power differential, one that will lead to an abuse of that power in relationship.

The man and the earth, with which he was created to be in harmony, are at odds, the outcome of their relationship uncertain, the fruits of their interactions now having the potential for both edification and frustration. So the circle of this first sin goes: the snake seeking truth, the woman and man seeking goodness and beauty, and all missing the mark, not because of their free will or the disease of sin, but because of the separation required for creation, the potential for all things to come to fruition and the continual becoming that will last into eternity.

Rather than God handing out punishments, their actions lead to the emergence of everything being more difficult, including relationship, procreation, survival, growing, eating, and working. They try for eternal possibilities—truth, beauty, and wisdom—and suffer, not because those things are bad, but because the way they went about it was to try to circumvent the process, to try to control the chaos at work around them and in them.

They yearned for these transcendent things and the overwhelming possibilities of creation bubbled up in them, so they reached out and took control of realizing that potential, but in a way that ended up being painful. They knew that they were transgressing the boundary that God had set. What they did was confuse the consequences of transgressing the boundary with the reason for the boundary itself. The snake was right that they would not die, the woman reached out knowing that they wouldn't, the man, seeing that the woman hadn't died, did the same, but they came to realize that God did not set up the boundary so that they wouldn't *die*, God set up the boundary so that they wouldn't *suffer*. Though, the story also makes clear, that the path of our life's journey is not avoiding suffering. We see that God does not necessarily cause suffering but God does not thwart it either. God, through creation, makes suffering possible and then responds through suffering to help us realize our potential, our depth, and the potential and depth of all of creation.

This Eden story is the illustration of the interactivity and reciprocity in the relationship between God and creation. There is a clear back and forth, actions and consequences for actions, possibilities and realized actualities, as God creates, creation responds to God, and God responds to creation. This is not the breaking down of creation's original intention, because the original intention was for creation to continue to become, to grow, and to increase in complexity and interconnection through the yearning for God. God sets up boundaries, boundaries that the very yearning for God leads humans to transgress, and then God responds. That response, though, is not through punishment, but through the natural consequence of relationship within creation, where God dwells. "The creature responds to the lure of the creator; the creator responds to the action of the creature. To respond is to become."[5] There is no becoming without action and there is no action, or interaction, with an impassive, distant, absolutely transcendent God. Such a view of God would be contrary to the illustration of God in this story, a story about the way creation and God continue to become through transgressive acts, addictions, and sins.

---

5. Keller, *Face of the Deep*, 198.

4

Addiction and Sin in Eden

In the throes of my addiction, I married someone who I had been dating since I was fifteen years old. We were comfortable, we had through traumatic family experiences, and, when I was twenty-one years old, it seemed like the logical next step in our relationship was to get married. I had convinced myself that checking off these boxes while I was so young would make me above reproach. On the outside, I worked hard to appear uninterested in what others thought about me. Internally, I was committed to being as perfect as possible, an upstanding Christian and citizen. My persona was one of a grounded, driven, focused, and faithful husband and priest-to-be who had it all figured out. I doled out advice to my peers with authority and confidence. I would be married, earn a Master's degree, be ordained, and be settled into my lifelong career before I was twenty-six. Beat that.

I was the picture of morality and used it to prop up my ego, hiding behind the "humble" persona of a servant. My outsides shone brightly in the eyes of those closest to me, but on the inside I was rotting away, moving further and further out of touch with any real relationship. I watched pornography every day. I fantasized about women in media and women in my everyday life. I obsessed about other people's bodies. I was always testing the waters of intimacy outside of my marriage. I was too scared to have a physical relationship with someone else, but I was always testing the boundaries of friendship. I kept all this hidden behind the façade of morality. I watched endless pornography while my wife and I took the moral high-ground of "waiting for marriage."

This worked, in one way or another, until it didn't. In December of 2011, I was twenty-three years old and watching pornography multiple times a day.

I had been married for a year and a half, and over the course of our eight-year relationship my wife had asked me multiple times if I watched porn and every time I lied. "No, never," I would say, "I don't do that." To make it even more convincing I would even sometimes become indignant for being asked, responding to her questions as if they were so preposterous that they did not even deserve an answer. Lying through my teeth, hoping against hope to never be found out, scared to death that I would be. Convinced that if I got caught I would surely die, the world would end, and my life would be over.

When that did happen, the world didn't end, my life wasn't ended, but life as I had known it, the world as I had known it, was over. The illusion of control, of my control over outcomes and possibilities, died that day. The chaos of relationship, which I had worked so hard to subdue, to dominate, to control, burst forth in a flood of suffering and half-truths. My wife caught me watching pornography one day in December 2011. She ran out of the room, and in complete shock I just sat there, trying to figure out what the hell I was going to do. I erased my search history and waited for her to come back. When she did, it began a months-long string of painful conversations. She was angry, hurt, and appalled at my actions. Though it was an opportunity to tell the truth, to tell my truth, I told her only as much as she already knew. "I only watch it sometimes," I would say, "barely ever." I exerted whatever final control I had and clung to my addiction for dear life.

She made it clear that she didn't want me to watch it anymore, and I told her that I would stop. I told myself that I would stop for her sake. What I learned is that trying to stop an addictive behavior for someone else does not work. I was just as addicted as before, I was just more obsessive and shamed about it. I told myself I wouldn't watch pornography, except for some nude pictures and videos. As long as there wasn't any sexual intercourse going on it didn't count. What I didn't know then was that stopping for her would not work because I was still in denial about my own suffering and unwilling to engage with the turmoil inside of me. I would not be able to stop until I could engage honestly with the suffering addiction was causing me. It had to come from inside out, not the other way around.

Creation in Relationship

If the first creation story in Genesis is about the nature of creation, the second creation story is about the nature of relationship within creation. It is a story about the quality of creation, the quality of relationship between the various parts of creation, and the consequences of bringing about difference and thus relationship within creation. It is a story about the potentials of all the various parts of creation and the chaotic depth of the relationships between them. Once things were made to be different, relationship was created, and implicit in relationship is this quality of chaos and the potential for an infinite number of outcomes.

The deception of one creature was not the origin of sin, the origin of sin was creation itself, separated from that original muck and made into different creatures all in relationship with God and one another. All of creation, from this first separation, yearns for relationship. The earth and water were in relationship. From their relationship emerged a human, and thus another relationship. Then two humans were made from this one, and all the rest of the created order followed, each an addition to the infinitely emerging web of relationships in creation. With each differentiation of creation, each new creature, a new relationship was created that held within it the potential for both suffering and joy, peace and enmity, and every outcome in between.

This conversation, a relationship, between a snake seeking truth and a woman seeking beauty and wisdom, ends in suffering, but also in the ability to be more deeply known and to know. From the spring of chaos flowed difference as it mixed with the earth to form the raw material of the different creatures. From difference, from relationship, the potential for both joy and suffering emerged. It was not from a deviant byproduct of free will, or the devil incarnate in a snake, but the realized potential of relationship.

If we strip away our preconceptions about these characters and neutralize our assumptions about their motivations, this story of Eden reveals itself to be something more than a narrative about how the origin of human sin came through an original act of transgression. What we see instead is a dramatic metaphor for the unbounded potentiality of creation in relationship and the suffering that flows from it. We see the unpredictability of outcomes from relations between parts of creation, and the bottomless desire of all parts of creation for deeper knowledge of God, creation, and self.

Eden, Addiction, and Sin

Instances of addiction, of sin, are not stains on our otherwise clean humanity, they are not road blocks on an otherwise clear path to wholeness, they *are* the path. They are the fabric of our humanity, not the stains on it. We are formed from the primordial muck, opened up inside by the breath of God, the breath that we still breathe today. We are made from the raw material of possibility, potential for outcomes joyful, painful, and mundane. We are made from the same muck but differentiated in that creation and inherently then flung into the chaotic potential of relationship with every part of creation. We are sent forth to transgress on a journey of knowing and being known, created to sin, to be addicted, always connected to that primordial chaos from which we came and still emerge. In our sin, in our addiction, we try to control these possibilities, these potentialities, this flow of inter-relationality. We try to control our relationship with parts of ourselves (sex addiction), with our own sense of peace (drugs and alcohol), with one another (codependence), with our own success (workaholism, competitiveness), with our anxiety (gambling, shopping, electronics), every time yearning to engage with all the infinite possibilities, and every time missing the mark by trying to take control.

Sin and addiction: these are one and the same thing, inextricably linked, one secular and one religious, but the same at the level of spirit, relationship, and experience. In addiction, we aim at that mark of relationship, with ourselves, one another, God, and the immense possibilities of those relationships that find their potential in our own depth, which is also the depth of God. We miss by trying to control instead of *letting be,* gently holding this chaos in us, letting it emerge in our lives and in relationship, letting it grow in us our potential, our power that is at the same time powerlessness. We are powerless in the face of the power of this chaos, this depth that is the depth of God in us, and yet this powerlessness can lead us to the letting be that cultivates in us a new kind of power, that is the co-creating with chaos that we have always been called to in every moment. It is this co-creating that leads us to become what we are called to become, to ever-emerging wholeness, to a putting back together of our God-given image, which is never set in stone but always emerging in relationship with everything.

This is the story of Eden, a story that shows that transgression is not a detour on our road to salvation but is the road itself, and leads to deeper knowing and engagement with reality, chaos, relationship, suffering, and God. It is a story of what happens when we are addicted, or sin, and how it is not a deviation from our creation, but a beloved part of it, necessary for our journey, indicative of our connection to God and the possibilities of relationship with the divine. We miss the mark in addiction, but instead of seeing it as indicative of our poor aim, it is indicative of the fact that we are aiming at the mark in the first place.

Like the woman in the story, we are all yearning for satisfaction, beauty, and wisdom, but we look for it in the wrong places, in the places that cause us pain. None of these yearnings are deceitful or evil. What we find is that when we reach out and grasp at these things, through our various addictive behaviors, we feel the pain of missing the mark. Our attempts are at those things that are transcendent but that can only be found in relationship. We each have our tree, our fruit. We each try to circumvent the spiritual journey to satisfaction, beauty, and wisdom by reaching out and grasping at those things that seem like the answer in the moment but end up causing us pain. Though, paradoxically, it is the actions themselves, and the suffering that ensues, that brings us into deeper relationship. It puts us in touch with the chaos within us that we are trying to grasp, but that we really need to let grasp us.

True peace and satisfaction is not something we can control and create ourselves, it can only happen in relationship. True beauty is not the perfection of reality but being able to recognize the reality of what is. True wisdom is not possible on our own, not something we can simply reach out and have, it is developed through relationship. Only through engaging with relationship and the depth of inter-relationality that is God, can we become that for which we are yearning and yearns for us. What we need to realize is that these painful behaviors, these addictions, these sins are not deviations from our spiritual journey, they *are* the spiritual journey.

The woman and man eating the fruit in Eden was both the first addictive behavior, the first sin, and, paradoxically, the necessary first step on the journey to depth, wisdom, satisfaction, beauty, reality, and the unity in relationship with God, creation, and the self. It is counterintuitive to think that suffering, difficulty, and the complicating of circumstances are *necessary* on the spiritual journey, but the truth is that instead of things getting easier on each step we walk, they get harder. Our journey does not lead to an immunity to suffering, but the ability to engage with the suffering face to face. Instead of trying to control the possibilities we are able to hold them gently and let them be. Through addictive behaviors we cause suffering in our relationships, but that suffering, when engaged face to face, leads to a new depth of relationship.

The story of Eden is not about how humanity became diseased with sin, or about the failure of free will to do the will of God. It is about the co-arising of every part of creation and the inter-relationality that inter-penetrates each and every creature, connecting us in relationship to one another, to ourselves, and thus to God. "To know another is to participate in the construction of that other within the mirror play of shared context. But both are still happening in and through each other. Nor does context lend closure. The boundaries of a context are constructs. One context shades into the next, and the next. In truth and in uncertainty—the whole earth might come tangled in every local relation."[1]

The Depth of Relationship

The very nature of God is relational: "Beloved, let us love one another, because love is from God; everyone who loves is born of God and knows God. Whoever does not love does not know God, for *God is love*" (1 John 4:7–8). This passage from First John does not say "God is loving" or "God is the source of love," but that *God is love itself*, God is relationship itself. And what is more chaotic, deep, and overflowing with the possibilities of both joy and suffering than love? In loving relationship, in any relationship, there is a constant tension between connection and separation, dependence and independence, and distance and intimacy.

When we fall in love, all we want to do is become one with the person with whom we are in love. We want to break down any separation and let our independence dissolve into the complete union we yearn to have with one another. What we often don't realize in the face of love is that there is no sustainability, no room for growth, and no real knowing without separation. No matter what, as connected as we may be to another person, we are still two separate people. At the same time, complete separation in its absolute form, like an unwillingness or inability to be vulnerable and intimate, builds up impenetrable boundaries and cuts off connection at the head.

These two extremes of relationship, then, offer similar outcomes. One is an absolute separation of two selves without any possibility for vulnerability and connection. The other is a dissolution of two selves into one that leads to total fusion and enmeshment. Both lead to stasis, frustration, and suffering. One leaves so much separation that it is as if there is no relationship at all and thus no growth. The other removes all space for separation and thus individual growth as two selves dissolve into one. The challenge is

---

1. Keller, *Cloud of the Impossible*, 21.

to find the third way between this "absolute and dissolute," which Catherine Keller describes as the "resolute."[2]

For relationship to happen there must both be a separation and a connection, two solid selves remaining in intimate and vulnerable union with one another. God, in creating all that is from this deep ocean of relationship and love, made things *different and separate.* In separating things, the dark from the light, the waters from the waters, the night from the day, the wet from the dry, and, in the second creation narrative, the one human into two, created the possibility of relationship in creation. This chaos, the source and possibility of difference, while it can lead us to both suffering or joy, is necessarily the source of relationship. It is this separation, this built-in tension of being both separate and in perfect union with God, that creates in us the potentials for co-creating both joy and suffering.

Our wholeness, our healing, comes from our ability to re-engage with this chaos in us. Our suffering comes from our innate ability to try to control it ourselves, to make ourselves completely separate and self-sufficient in our independence from God. But this re-engaging with chaos puts us back in touch with the tension of this dependence and independence and leads us to an ability to recognize our *interdependence* in relationship to God, to one another, and to all of creation. We are not wholly self-sufficient (independent) in our ability to function in creation, but we also are not wholly insufficient (dependent) in our journey of growth and transformation. This is the third way between the views of Pelagius (independent/ self-sufficient) and Augustine (dependent/insufficient) in the conversation about God's grace. We find ourselves in a third place, where we have this ability in our humanity to forget our connection, to try to take over control and to ignore our connection to God. This ability, though, also leads us back to the realization of that union and into a co-creative role of interdependence with the divine.

Keller notes of this tehomic depth that she "would not, however, call it God, but *the depth of God,* . . . the heterogeneous depth of divinity and of world . . . ."[3] From the depth of God comes difference, the separation that makes relationship possible and makes love possible. It is here that we find the answer to our questions of why. Why do we have to be separate? Why is this our journey? Like a child in the womb, we were completely connected to our source of life and provided with everything we needed to grow and

2. Keller, *On the Mystery,* 25.
3. Keller, *Face of the Deep,* 231.

thrive. Why couldn't we have just stayed in Eden, where all our needs were met, where we were in complete and utter union with God, and where we could relate to God directly and more intimately than we would ever be able to again?

A New Birth

Humanity could never have stayed in Eden. It is finite, bounded, and there is nothing about creation that is finite. Creation cannot help but burst at the seams, continue to become, to grow, to be more and more. If creation stopped becoming, growing, transforming, changing, it would no longer be creation. Eden is not the destination, it was just the beginning, and it was no more the goal to stay in Eden that it is the goal for us to have stayed in the womb. Yes, we had everything we needed, but it was small, dark, and only a speck of space in the midst of creation, and we can only spend so much time there before we grow too big for its comfortable confines. Further still, it is no more our hope to return to Eden, or even possible to, than it is to return to the womb.

The question that Nicodemus asks Jesus in John's Gospel echoes here,

> "How can anyone be born after having grown old? Can one enter a second time into the mother's womb and be born?" Jesus answered, "Very truly, I tell you, no one can enter the kingdom of God without being born of water and Spirit. What is born of the flesh is flesh, and what is born of the Spirit is spirit. Do not be astonished that I said to you, 'You must be born from above.' The wind blows where it chooses, and you hear the sound of it, but you do not know where it comes from or where it goes. So it is with everyone who is born of the Spirit." (John 3:4–8)

It is a different kind of birth altogether of which Jesus speaks.

This is not a once-and-for-all birth, but indicative of what is happening for us all the time. Each act of sin, each act of addiction is a new expulsion from the illusion of control, of boundaries, of the finite, and of our separation. Adam and Eve don't get expelled from Eden in that they are kicked out of a place that still exists but they can't get back into. Rather, the boundaries of Eden, the illusion of the idyllic, are shown to be what they truly are. Each addiction is a new birth into a deeper way of knowing beyond knowing, and new births are happening all the time; births, like Jesus describes, "of water and Spirit" (John 3:8).

This birth into the world beyond the boundaries of Eden was the necessary next step in the relationship between humanity and God. It is the same as how a mother is completely connected to her child in every way as she waits expectantly for its birth, but there is still a barrier to their relationship. In this absence of separation, this complete union where one lives *inside* the other, there is a limit to how much the mother can know the child. The baby cannot be fully known by the mother, the source of life, the creator, while she or he is still in the womb and fully connected. As a baby is born into the world, Adam and Eve were cast into the toil of life beyond Eden, removed from the warmth and safety of the womb, but finally in a place where they could be known by God in relationship. Though they were then vulnerable to both joy and suffering, and to the chaos of life that brings forth possibilities of all kinds, it is only out there that they could grow, that they could be in relationship, and risk being known.

It is only outside of Eden that God can know us, that we can be known by God and know God in any way. There was enmeshment in the womb of Eden, but we can only be known so much by poking and prodding though the belly. It is only after we emerge into the world, where we can suffer and cause suffering, feel joy and create joy, that we can know God and be known. It is our addictions, what we see as sins in Eden, that facilitate our reconnection to that depth, removed from enmeshment (dependence), brought to our knees by our attempts to control (independence) and back to joyful re-engagement with our chaos, where we are held and participate in our becoming (interdependence) with God and the rest of creation.

We can only engage with the chaos of the world when we leave Eden. Eden is an illusion in the midst of real, gritty, chaotic creation. It is this tiny portion of a wider world that is not as comfortable and safe but leads to actual relationship, growth, transformation, and the ability to reconnect to our humanity, our ʿāphār-ness, and to God. It is hard out here, but it is real. Without the transgression of eating from the tree, there would be nowhere for creation to grow. It would be stuck, and creation is never stuck. Just like us, it is always moving, becoming, and changing. At some point we realize we are yearning for something more, and we look for it in places that cause us pain, but that ultimately reconnect us to our chaos and our union with God. Our addictions open the door out of Eden and this is a grace of God, to be able to move beyond the small self, the Edenic environment, and into engagement with the entirety of creation, with all of its potential for joy and suffering, pain and comfort, fear and peace. It is a peace that is

49

not the absence of chaos or the negation of discomfort, but an ability to sit quietly and lovingly with our chaos and discomfort. Not only that, but it can cultivate in us the ability to befriend it, engage with it compassionately, and gently let it be what it will be.

Reaching Out and Grasping

This story of Eden has been the source of our disease model of sin for over fifteen hundred years. Through it theologians like Augustine of Hippo have argued that there is something infecting our once good humanity, and that we are in need of a physician to treat it. Augustine's inclination toward using this story to illustrate qualities of God's grace was well founded, but rather than this being a story about *why* God's grace works in our lives, it is much more a story about *how* God's grace works in our lives. Rather than God's grace working *against* sin, God's grace works *through* sin, which shows itself to be a tool for our growth and transformation. From the very beginning, this story shows us that it is part of our created being to be able to miss the mark. The serpent, the tree, the woman, the man: all were created by God and every part of them was created by God. Nothing happened in this story that was not made possible by the way God created all of these things. This is not the story of our fall from grace. It is the story of how our journey works, and how grace works in us.

While there is suffering brought forth by the various actions and relationships in the story, all these things work toward the creation of a newness in relationship and a new kind of knowing and being known. Like our addictions, these original sins of Eden do cause pain and suffering, but they also create new depth in relationship, new possibilities for knowing and being known between the various parts of creation and God. They are an invitation to recognize the interdependence of all of creation, the way that everything is connected, and thus to engage with the dynamic chaos both within and without. Through the human impulse for independence these characters reach out and try to grasp the eternal themselves, to take control of these dynamics swirling in and around them. The effects of their actions are immediate, as they come to realize and engage with their reality in a new way.

Eden shows us that the original sin, which is addiction, is the reaching out and grasping that leads to suffering. This, though, was not a deviation from God's intention for us. Rather, this suffering is what emerges naturally from relationship, which produces the chaos which we try to control. Then it is through this suffering that we continue to deepen that relationship, that we are able to grow in our own depths, that we are able to know God and thus rediscover our connection to God. This story—which is the foundation for how we understand our spiritual journey, humanity, sin, and suffering—is not a story of evil and deception. Instead, it reveals that "illimitable interactivity"[4] of creation that is only born through suffering and engagement with suffering. It illustrates that our journey is to let this chaotic depth wash over us and recreate us. We need to breathe it in like amniotic fluid, giving us all the life and nutrients we need to grow and transform, and not fight our submergence but allow ourselves to float in the ebb and flow of the chaotic river of multiplicity, impossibility, and reality.

Held side by side, do these two concepts—addiction and sin—begin to lose their distinction? Both are attempts at something eternal, both are misses, both are ways we try to control our chaos, both are indications of our union with the divine. Might these "diseases" be one in the same? Addiction and sin give way to addiction/sin: the experience of yearning, trying, missing, and by grace being brought to deeper connection with God, with our chaos, with our potential, our possibilities, and our greatest source of power. The parallel lives of sin and addiction are also indicative of a deeper connection between these two concepts. There is a reason that we find both understood, one in the secular world of science and twelve-step groups and one in the religious world of Christianity, as some kind of disease.

What difference can we discern then between what we call addiction and what we call sin? May they be one in the same phenomenon? To answer these questions, we must take a closer look at sin, where it comes from, how it has been explained, and where it is inviting us to go next in our understanding about ourselves, humanity, and God.

---

4. Keller, *On the Mystery*, 84.

5

Sin: Relative or Relational?

Slowly days turned into weeks and weeks into months and months into years and eventually everything seemed to be at peace again in our marriage. Well, I told myself everything was at peace. I told myself I was still okay. I told myself I wasn't addicted. I told myself I wasn't doing anything wrong. I had told enough truth to get back to some kind of normalcy and told enough lies to keep myself trapped for a little while longer. The August after this blowup I began a Master of Divinity program at Virginia Theological Seminary. I had been in the ordination process for two years and was on my way to becoming an Episcopal priest.

As I continued through school and moved deeper into the process of becoming a priest a few slivers of light began to show in the walls of my cell. The mortar between the bricks began to crumble and walls that I had built began to crack and shift around me. I moved into the summer after my first year of school still thinking I had it under control, but I also began to have the thought that maybe I was addicted to pornography. I knew of Alcoholics Anonymous programs and twelve-step programs for other addictions, and I wondered to myself if there were such programs for pornography. I did not go so far as searching them out though, at least not then. I still wasn't ready to admit defeat.

In the summer of 2013, following my first year of school, I took part in a ten-week chaplaincy program at a hospital in Fredericksburg, Virginia as part of a mandatory requirement for ordination. The program, referred to as CPE (Clinical Pastoral Education) was a chaplaincy internship, which was meant to equip participants with the tools to do pastoral care. At the hospital, I was assigned to a floor of patient rooms where I would spend most of my days for ten weeks visiting patients in order to provide any kind of spiritual and pastoral support I could while they were in the hospital.

The program also included focused group and one-on-one supervisory time, where we spent hours reviewing these pastoral care interactions and reflecting on our own inner journey along the way. This was the first time that I had been in such a setting. It was the first time that I had been asked to take seriously what was going on inside of me. It was the first time that I had been asked to gaze deeply at places of pain in my life, hold them gently, and wonder how they were affecting my ability to connect with people. I had never been faced with my disconnection, and when I was I could feel the foundation begin to shift underneath me.

Through this experience I realized for the first time the width and depth of the chasm that had formed between me and everyone in my life, both people I had known forever and people I was meeting anew every day. I was being asked to sit with people in their pain, anxiety, and fear and connect with them from the level of my own. Each interaction and subsequent reflection was a new indication of how far away I was from everyone else. It was an indication of how separated I was from the depths of myself, the depths of my life experience, and the depths of the world around me. Every day was another hammer stroke clanging against the walls I had built inside, and it was only a matter of time until it all fell down.

The Weapon of Sin

Just as the Alcoholics Anonymous language of disease in the 1950s was a starting point for understanding addiction, so too was Augustine's fifth-century disease model of sin a starting point at which we still find ourselves stuck. In 1957, Lutheran Theologian Paul Tillich took on a similar linguistic challenge by critiquing the modern use of the term "faith." In the face of what he saw as a continued distortion in the understanding of the term faith in Christianity, he wrote the following in his book *Dynamics of Faith*:

> There is hardly a word in the religious language, both theological and popular, which is subject to more misunderstandings, distortions and questionable definitions than the word "faith." It belongs to those terms which need healing before they can be used for the healing of [people]. Today the term "faith" is more productive of disease than of health. It confuses, misleads, creates alternately

skepticism and fanaticism, intellectual resistance and emotional surrender, rejection of genuine religion and subjection to sub- stitutes. Indeed, one is tempted to suggest that the word "faith" should be dropped completely; but desirable as that may be it is hardly possible. A powerful tradition protects it. And there is as yet no substitute expressing the reality to which the term "faith" points. So, for the time being the only way of dealing with the problem is to try to reinterpret the word and remove the confu- sion and distorting connotations, some of which are the heritage of centuries.[1]

One of Tillich's main assertions is that the opposite of faith is not doubt but certainty, and that defining faith as a person's certainty in a set of beliefs was not only a distortion of the term but detrimental to our spiritual growth and formation. For Tillich, redefining faith in this way made it an invitational tool for the spiritual journey rather than a rigid theological weapon. A weapon too often used by those claiming religious certainty to bash those who admitted to having any doubts in their faith.

As discussed in the previous chapter, the concept of sin also "belongs to those terms which need healing before they can be used for the healing of [people]."[2] Thus far, we have explored the concept of original sin, the Au- gustinian theology from which a disease model of sin has developed within the Christian tradition, and the creation story from which it emerged. The concept of original sin may have provided the theological foundation for understanding humanity as in some way diseased, but there is another facet to our popular understanding of sin in the twenty-first century. Augustine's interpretation of the first sin of Adam and Eve in the garden of Eden solidi- fied the idea that our humanity in and of itself is infected with sin. Today our conversation about sin is much more focused on individual behaviors that we categorize as sin than on the inherently sinful nature of humanity. It is the individual sin that has become the focus of religious morality. This is the theological environment we now find ourselves in, where there is an overemphasis on individual behavior rather than on better understanding our common humanity.

This is part of a larger trend, especially in the Western Christian theological tradition, of emphasizing individual salvation over universal salvation as the call of the gospel. Because of this obsession with individual behavior as the focus of our theology of sin, the concept has taken on all the

1. Tillich, *Dynamics of Faith*, ix.
2. Tillich, *Dynamics of Faith*, ix.

trappings of shame and guilt that come with conservative morality. Thus, the term sin has been largely taken over by a particular conservative part of the Christian tradition that is obsessed with other people's behaviors, especially sexual behaviors, in order to shame others into believing, acting, and living the way that they want them to live.

Now, as we move further into the twenty-first century, there is an entire generation (if not multiple generations) of people for whom the word "sin" has been used as a weapon with which to cut them down and shame them into compliance. Thus, we have lost the ability to speak openly about sin, to use it constructively and to be able to relate with one another about it. Either it is overused by those of a more conservative, absolutist tradition as a weapon, actively resisted by those who have been so attacked with the word for so long that its mention is enough to shut down conversation in its tracks, or avoided by those of a more progressive theological tradition out of fear that its mention will reopen the wounds caused by its use as a weapon.

This is a far cry from Augustine's intention in writing about sin in the fifth century. Where has God's grace gone in the battle for theological and moral supremacy? If we silence conversation about sin, about the ways we are hurting, about the conditions of our humanity, we silence any conversation about God's grace working in our lives. As we have lost the ability to speak openly about sin, sin has lost its transformational and healing properties. Because it carries with it such great power, sin has often been hijacked and used as a weapon. The power of the word is not unwarranted, for it belongs to those terms that find deep roots in the Christian theological tradition, and "there is as yet no substitute expressing the reality to which [it] points."[3] Faced with all of the spiritual, emotional, and physical trauma that has been caused by sin, it would be nice to be able to throw it out completely, tear it out, root and limb, from the ground of the tradition as if it never existed, never passed through the lips of a single person, spat out like a burning stamp of judgment onto another. Not only is this impossible, but wouldn't this just be the theological equivalent of that surgical removal of disease explored in chapter 1, excising the parts, either of ourselves or of the Christian tradition, that we don't like, thinking that some parts are good, and some parts are bad?

Instead, in the hopes of preserving and redirecting the great power we find in the concept of sin, let us attempt to explore its depths in a way that

3. Tillich, *Dynamics of Faith*, ix.

may lead to its transformation before our eyes from a violent weapon into a powerful tool used to cultivate in us fertile ground for our own growth and transformation. Maybe we can do the work of turning these theological weapons into tools, of turning "swords into plowshares," and "spears into pruning hooks" (Isa 2:4). Maybe we can recapture the great power of sin as a tool for growth. After all, like any concept it can only carry great power if it is rooted in truth. And it can only be rooted in truth if it speaks to love, the deepest truth of all.

There can be no discussion about sin removed from God's eternal and overflowing love for humanity, for all of creation and for each and every one of us. As much as Paul Tillich recognized the desperate need to reframe faith for the twentieth century, we must recognize and respond to the need to reframe sin for the twenty-first century. Sin is a vital part of our spiritual journey, but only if we are able "to reinterpret the word and remove the confusion and distorting connotations, some of which are the heritage of centuries."[4]

Missing the Mark

Often, we think of a sin as a behavior that is one of many on a laundry list of behaviors that God doesn't like, or that are offensive to God. We also tend to think of sin as something dark and evil that lives inside of us, as some sort of penchant for our own destruction that we must rebel against and ask God constantly to remove. Sin, popularly understood, is a twofold idea. First, it is the remnant of that original sin in the garden of Eden that began with Adam and Eve, has been passed down, and infects all of humanity. Second, from this sin-disease come individual sins, or behaviors that we partake in as humans that are on the extensive list of (seemingly arbitrary) behaviors that God does not approve of, and for which we will eventually be punished. This is the context within which we currently also talk about the behaviors of various addictions, whether we are aware of it or not.

As discussed in the previous chapter, much of our current approach to understanding sin is based on the theological writings of Augustine. He, though, is a natural theological successor to the most prolific writer of New Testament works, Paul, who wrote at least seven of the twenty-seven books that comprise the New Testament and possibly as many as fourteen. Paul wrote extensively about sin, and specifically in relation to his understanding

4. Tillich, *Dynamics of Faith*, ix.

of the saving work of Jesus' death and resurrection, referred to in theology as soteriology, or theology of salvation (*sōtēria* in Greek).

The Greek word used by Paul, and the other New Testament authors, that we today translate as sin was the word *hamartia*, which came from the verb *hamartano*, translated today as "to sin." *Hamartano* carried a very specific milieu of meaning in the first century. In its original Greek context, *hamartano* meant "to miss a definite goal," and, as a term originally used among archers, meant more specifically "to miss the mark." *Hamartia* then was the action of missing the target, aiming at a goal and missing it. Stripping away the centuries of moralism that have been layered on top of this word, what emerges is not an action that in and of itself implies evil intentions or bad behavior. It is only "bad" in that the hope is always to hit the mark, and to miss it means to not achieve the initial aim of the behavior.

Instead of thinking about a sin as a behavior that God will punish us for, an arbitrary rule outlined in the Bible that we are not to transgress, this theology of missing the mark has deep implications for our spiritual lives and the overwhelming yearning for God. We often focus our attention on the missing that happens in sin, on the behaviors and their consequences, and indeed these are important. But before there is a miss, before there is a behavior and a consequence, there must first be a mark, a target at which we are aiming. Rather than devolving into shame and guilt over the act of missing, what if we instead turned our attention to the fact that there is a mark in the first place, and that every errant attempt is a way to learn something about why we miss, an invitation to shift our aim, and a reminder that our sins are indicative of aiming not at evil targets but at transcendent ones?

What Is the Mark?

In its United States Catechism for Adults, the Catholic Church defines sin as "an offense against God as well as neighbor and therefore wrong."[5] This definition follows from a quote by Augustine found in his *Contra Faustum* defining sin as "an utterance, deed, or a desire contrary to the eternal law."[6] The Episcopal Church, in the Book of Common Prayer catechism, defines

5. Catholic Church United States Conference of Catholic Bishops, *United States Catholic Catechism for Adults*, 637.

6. Catholic Church United States Conference of Catholic Bishops, *United States Catholic Catechism for Adults*, 312.

sin as "the seeking of our own will instead of the will of God."[7] These definitions paint a very specific picture of a Western view of sin in which to "miss the mark" is to not follow "the eternal law," "the will of God," and thus to commit an "offense against God." In order to avoid sin, which would seem like the point of the whole religious life, mustn't we first know exactly what behaviors this law encompasses and therefore what is and is not an offense? Often, what one defines as the law changes depending on the particular religious tradition and context within which one finds themselves. Is the law the Ten Commandments? Or is it the Ten Commandments plus the hundreds of other laws found in the Hebrew scriptures? Or is it the Ten Commandments, the hundreds of laws, and the commandments of Jesus reported in the Gospels? Or is it the Ten Commandments, the hundreds of laws, Jesus' commandments, and any commandments from Paul, Pseudo-Paul, or other writers of non-Gospel books in the New Testament?

For the sake of simplicity, let's say that we are concerned only with the Ten Commandments found in the book of Exodus. In the case of the Ten Commandments, to miss the mark would mean to perform one of these ten behaviors that God has commanded humanity not to perform. Therefore, the law is the mark and to miss it would be to behave in one of the ten specific ways in which we are not supposed to. But what *is* the law? What is its intention? Why is the law the mark? Removed from human experience and human suffering, the law is arbitrary, dead, and weaponized. Instead of a list of behaviors that God has decided are wrong, or offensive, or that God doesn't like, is there something deeper to them than meets the eye? What if, instead of ten arbitrary rules, these commandments are safeguards against suffering? To break any single one of them is painful, not because it is painful to break a rule, but because the actions *in and of themselves* lead to suffering.

The Ten Commandments outline painful behaviors, such as separation from God, idolatry, desecration, overwork, family cut-off, murder, adultery, lying, and coveting. These aren't arbitrary rules, this is a list of the most deeply painful behaviors in which we can engage. The Ten Commandments are not a list of behaviors God created so God could punish us. They are not the mark in and of themselves. They are a list of *misses*, not targets. If the Ten Commandments didn't exist, if they had never been carved into stone, if they had never been transmitted to us over thousands of years, these behaviors would *still* be painful. Simply *keeping* the law can't be the

7. Episcopal Church, *The Book of Common Prayer*, 848.

target, because if that were the case these things would cease to be painful if they were not forbidden. Rather, idolatry is painful, coveting is painful, murder is painful, adultery is painful, not honoring family is painful. The Ten Commandments are a list of ten ways we miss the mark, ten ways that we sin. The law is not the mark, the mark is deeper than the law. The mark we miss is relationship: with God, with ourselves, and with one another.

It is as if we walked into a room where an archer had just shot ten arrows at a target on a wall. The archer has gone and taken the target with her, though she has left ten arrows that missed the target stuck in the wall. Our task upon entering, without knowing anything about the placement of the target in the room and thus where the archer was aiming, is to determine as much about the target as possible. With the information we have, it is hard to know specific details about the target like its color, its texture, the material it is made of, or its size. What we do know is what the misses looked like. We can see where the archer missed the mark. By the *negative* space on the wall created by the missed arrows we can outline what the shape of the target *might* be and give a pretty good guess as to where the archer was aiming. Those arrows are the Ten Commandments, and though we have a limited capacity to know much about this mark, we can do the work of reconstructing what it is, based on the experience of missing it.

A Natural Theology of Sin

The list of what today constitutes a transgression, and thus a sin, in the eyes of various religious traditions, especially "conservative" ones, continues to grow. For some, it's consumption of alcohol; for some, pornography; for some, non-heterosexual relationships and sexual behavior; for some, drug use, or any other on a list of "sinful" behaviors that have grown over the last two thousand years of Christian history. Many of these are based either on very narrow interpretations of Scripture or not on Scripture at all. Often, these proscribed behaviors are based more on what makes the powerful majority uncomfortable than on anything else.

What if we defined sin not as an arbitrary behavior that causes God to become angry but as an action that causes us pain? How would this change the way we understand ourselves in relation to God and to the world? This alternative approach to sin is the product of a field called natural theology, which represents an area of theology whose chief concern is "the relationship between our mundane experience and ultimate reality."[8] Jessica Frazier, a lecturer in Religious Studies at the University of Kent, defines it specifically as "the process of discovering ultimate truths via the capacities (both empirical and logical) of the human mind, as opposed to relying only on revelation."[9] This is not to say that the "capacities of the human mind" and what we classically understand as revelation (i.e., the Bible) must necessarily stand in opposition to one another as possible sources of truth. Instead of competing, reason and revelation can complement each other. Those lessons learned from the human experience and the revelation of God through Scripture can be used together to create a textured theology wherein one source informs the other.

In a 2009 conference at the Center for Action and Contemplation, Franciscan Friar Richard Rohr emphasized personal experience as part of a natural theology of sin. Rohr suggested that "Sin isn't just something forbidden by God. Sin is that which doesn't work. Sin is self-defeating behavior. Sin messes you up. It's not *God* who doesn't like it, it's *you* who shouldn't like it. . . . We are not punished *for* our sins, which is the way we almost all think, we are punished *by* our sins."[10] Rohr's belief that we are "punished by our sins" rather than "for our sins" means that we do not need to rely on an arbitrary list of actions that offend God to be able to define sin. Rather than God punishing us for our actions, like an angry parent, we are punished in the moment we act, because sins hurt us right then and there in our immediate experience. Sins are not actions we should avoid because God doesn't like them and will become angry with us if we commit them, they are actions to avoid because they are painful, and God knows that they are painful. Sin is "self-defeating behavior," it is "that which doesn't work,"[11] and therefore we identify sins not by their inclusion on a list of behaviors but from the suffering that they cause in our lives.

As we continue to hammer on the sharp-edged weapon of sin, what begins to take shape before our eyes is that cultivating tool we so desperately need. If sin is not an offense punishable by a petty and irritable God and instead is a way of describing those actions we take that are painful and cause suffering within us, in our relationships, and in the world, then we have a path forward in our own re-union with the divine.

8. Frazier, "Natural Theology in Easter Religions," 167 .

9. Frazier, "Natural Theology in Easter Religions," 167.

10. Rohr, *Laughing and Weeping*. CD.

11. Rohr, *Laughing and Weeping*. CD.

Returning to the Ten Commandments, what are these laws created to safeguard? Is it God's attempt to protect Godself from being hurt by humanity? Or is it rather God's attempt to safeguard relationship, both with God and with one another? If this is so, have we not stumbled upon the target for which we have been searching? The mark that is missed in our sin is not the law, the mark is *relationship*, and not just the individual friendship, marriage, or kinship. It is the eternal essence of relationality, our ability to relate, to be in relationship to one another, to be able to remain connected to other people, to the world around us, and to ourselves. Not only that, but even more specifically, it is our ability to remain connected to that chaos, that depth, that is inter-relationality. The law exists to help us to remain connected to the chaos around us, in us, and between us.

The mark that is this eternal law is the engagement with the chaos of relationship and inter-relationship. Taking the Ten Commandments as an example, let's look at them as the ways we miss the mark of *engaging* with this chaotic depth of our experience, the depth of God. One of the ways we can miss is by making the overwhelming transcendence of God one dimensional (graven images), or trying to avoid direct relationship with this uncontrollable, ungraspable God by trying to make things we can control into gods (no other god before me). We avoid the chaos of resting, of silence and unproductive time (keep the Sabbath). We avoid the deeply complex (chaotic) dynamics of our relationships with our parents and other family members (honor father and mother). We lie about the ways we have caused suffering in our own lives and the lives of others (bear false witness). We continue to seek what we do not have instead of engaging with what is already within us (coveting). These are ways we miss the mark of relationship, God, and chaotic relationality, which we are always being invited back to through our sins. Missing the mark is painful, but it is also indicative that there is something at which we are aiming that is deeper than what meets the eye. It is our invitation to engage with our chaos, the depth of relation, which "remains neither God nor not-God but the depth of 'God'" and the "matrix of *all relations*."[12]

Sin Is Not Relative, It Is Relational

In this new model, sin is defined not as a preset list of behaviors that can be judged as sins from outside but rather as those behaviors that cause us

12. Keller, *Face of the Deep*, 227.

suffering and that are painful in the moment. Sin, then, is based on individual experience, rather than on holding up observable behavior against a measuring stick of law and morality. These laws engraved on stone tablets, passed down in long Levitical lists in Scripture and developed over two millennia of cultural acceptance cannot be the measuring stick with which we judge the behaviors of others. One might think that this means we descend into the murky non-claims of relativism, and in the hope of finding a transformational alternative to guilt-ridden theologies of sin we wander into the quicksand of relativity.

We are indeed moving away from a sense of supreme certainty in how we are supposed to behave and what, if anything, we can judge as good or evil in the eyes of God. Fortunately, it has never been and will never be our hope to be certain of anything. If the law in and of itself is not the target of our behavior, then we can no longer judge one another's behaviors externally based on the law. Instead, the goal of the law and thus the target of our behavior is relationality itself, relationship itself, our reengagement with the chaotic potential of our depths, what we might characterize as our union with God.

This need for certainty, though, is not born from a fear of relativism, where everyone has a claim to their own truth detached from some larger truth to which we are all connected. Instead, it is indicative of a lack of trust. If we can't be certain, based on a clearly defined set of rules, that someone else's behavior is good or bad, virtuous or sinful, acceptable or unacceptable, how can we be certain of anything? If we can't stand firmly on the moral ground of the law, what can we stand firmly on? If the law is not our target, then it is not the foundation on which we stand. Instead, relationship is the target, and *that* is the foundation for truth on which we can depend. First, though, we need to trust one another, and value a commitment to trust over a desperation for certainty. As Keller asserts, "Truth and *trust* are closely related words, as displayed in the archaic form of the word for truth, 'troth,' as in 'to pledge your troth.' 'Truth' at its root signifies a covenant of trustworthiness, in a marriage contract. To be true to another means to be trusty!"[13]

If the truth of sin is not based on external law, but instead on trusting one another's experience, then the truth of sin is not relative but *relational*. Being able to discern what is a sin and what is not is not up to anyone but

---

13. Keller, *On the Mystery*, 37.

the sinner. If we are "punished by our sins" rather than "for our sins"[14] then the consequence for and indication of sin is not an impending punishment but suffering in the moment. Knowing what a sin is can only happen in relating, in relationship, and in sharing the truth of our experience with one another. Keller's relationality rings true here, "Faith in these stories, in these relations of hearing, of risky self-disclosure, of facing fear, lets us step forward in mystery. This step would be 'faith' in the New Testament sense of *pistis,* 'trust,' and precisely not 'belief' as a proposition or a prescription."[15] This truth is a mystery, not in that it is impossible to know, but that it is impossible to define once and for all outside of continuous, emerging, and ever-transforming relationship. It "has little to do with right or wrong belief or dogma; nor is it some eternal verity engraved in our souls; it is a truth of right relation, to be embodied and enacted."[16]

The corrective action of relationality goes both ways, transforming both humanity as it has experiences and the law itself. Returning to our example of the Ten Commandments, those "thou shalts" and "thou shalt nots" are indicative of actions that ultimately cause us suffering, and often cause the suffering of others as well. If there is a law, though, that does not prove to be safeguarding us from suffering, then the law is as much in need of correction as we are. This is a natural consequence of the authority of our experience balancing the authority of revelation in Scripture. "*To continue* in this truth, in this relationality, requires the critical fidelity that tests any testimony. Truth does not transcend its context but changes it. . . . The truth-path is not liberation *from* the world but *in* it."[17] This is the path, the path of co-arising inter-relationality, where if we do not recognize the interplay between these various parts of creation, including the law, and the way in which everything is transforming and becoming, then we are living in an illusion.

There is no certainty, no knowing, outside of relationship, because even those things that are eternal, like God, the law, and truth, are themselves in a continual state of being revealed. "This truth of faithful relationality in which we are called to walk and talk has everything to do with con/sciousness ('knowing *with*') and nothing to do with certainty."[18] There is no

14. Rohr, *Laughing and Weeping.* CD.

15. Keller, *On the Mystery,* 208.

16. Keller, *On the Mystery,* 208.

17. Keller, *On the Mystery,* 43.

18. Keller, *On the Mystery,* 38.

knowing outside of "knowing with," and there is no "knowing with" outside of relationship. There is no relationship when our interactions begin and end with the judgment of others, born out of a fear for the unknown.

> Nothing in other words is known outside of relation—whether of terror, tedium, or love. Nothing knowable comes constructed *ex nihilo,* void of context. If something is known at all, it cannot be absolved of relation; therefore nothing is known ab-solutely. Not God, not me, not you, not truth, not justice, not Earth, not flesh, not photon. Each is what it is only in relation to its others.[19]

Moses and the Cloud

Consider the story of Moses on Mount Sinai when the Ten Commandments were handed down to the people by God. The Exodus account of Moses receiving the commandments describes God descending on Mount Sinai in a "thick cloud" (Exod 19:16) with tremendous sounds and that only Moses was allowed to meet God on the mountain on behalf of all the people. When God revealed the law to Moses "the people witnessed the thunder and lightning, the sound of the trumpet, and the mountain smoking, they were afraid and trembled and stood at a distance" (Exod 20:18). Then they said to Moses, "You speak to us, and we will listen; but do not let God speak to us, or we will die" (Exod 20:19). In this episode we see the way that God reveals God's self and the trust needed in relationship for the truth of God to be revealed to the world. God descends on the cloud, not as a form, not with a face, but in a dark cloud, where Moses experiences God, but does not know God face to face. Instead, Moses experiences this cloud, this ungraspable reality, where the law is revealed to him, and (through him) to the people he is in relationship with, gathered at the bottom of the mountain. "In this *tremendum,* in awe or terror, they must trust Moses to translate."[20]

We all experience God like Moses does on Mount Sinai, in an ungraspable cloud of thick darkness, where we know and unknow at the same time. We experience God in relationship with others, the cloud of our interrelationship, made up of the infinite network of relationships within which we all "live and move and have our being" (Acts 17:28). We experience

19. Keller, *Cloud of the Impossible,* 21.
20. Keller, *Cloud of the Impossible,* 152.

God, in joy or suffering, in experiences that lead to pain or peace, and then we must, like the Israelites at the foot of Mount Sinai, trust one another to translate this experience. This is the role of trust in truth, in our ability to "know-with"[21] one another through relationship. Moses experiences God on Mount Sinai and translates this experience for the people into the Ten Commandments, the ten ways that we cause suffering, for ourselves and for one another.

This is the process in which we must trust to remain connected in truth and trust and grow in relationship to one another. We know the truth of sin, the truth of suffering, the truth of addiction only in relationship and only in trusting one another. This is why we cannot rely on external judgment to "diagnose" someone as a sinner. This is why we cannot use the Ten Commandments, or the law, or whatever list of moral behaviors we draw from to measure other people's behavior, to define what sin is for someone else. All we can do is trust one another to translate their experience of God, this unknowable, ungraspable cloud of relationality and experience, and share what is causing suffering in their lives.

When we define sin as that which doesn't work, as those behaviors that cause us to suffer, rather than a list of actions forbidden by God, we enter together into this thick cloud that is neither moral absolutism nor moral relativism. It is the cloud of relationality within which God descends in the experiences of our lives. Since we cannot know someone else's suffering any more that we can know God, all we can do is trust others to share with us what has caused suffering in their lives and what they understand as their sinful behaviors.

Take any of the behaviors that get targeted as sinful by a moral absolutism; drinking, sex, non-heterosexual relationships, drug use. I do not get to label any of these behaviors as sins. I am called, instead, to be in relationship with people and bear witness to what is causing suffering in their lives and trust them when they reveal what does and does not cause suffering for them. There is a large swath of Christianity that wants desperately to label any and all non-heterosexual relationships as sinful, but I cannot know sin outside of relationship with people, and only then can I bear witness to sin when someone shares with me something that is causing them suffering. Outside of actions that are causing direct harm to another person through violence or oppression, if a behavior is not causing a person to suffer then it is not a sin, and I must trust each and every person to translate their

21. Keller, On the Mystery, 38.

experience to me and believe them when they say that something either is or is not causing them suffering. There is no knowing outside of "knowing with,"[22] no truth outside of relationship and no sin outside of suffering.

When we walk around telling people that they are sinners, that their behaviors are sinful, we are missing the mark of that "eternal law"[23] of Augustine, which is relationship, and trust in relationship. We don't get to tell people that they are sinners, that they have sinned, they get to tell us. We can only tell one another, translate our experience of the thick cloud, when we can stay connected, when we can remain engaged with this chaotic depth in us and around us that is the cloud of our interconnected relationships, the depth of God.

Addiction and the Mark

This understanding of sin is the model for how we are invited to understand addiction in a new way. In addiction, my deepest desire is to be completely connected and in tune with my own depth and the depth of God in me, a depth of union in which I cannot tell where I end and God begins. In sex addiction and in pornography I am connecting with that deep desire and trying desperately to answer the call of that deep transcendent yearning but doing it in ways that ultimately cause me harm and suffering. This is not to say that sex is evil, or that there is no point to sexuality and relationship with another person if my ultimate yearning is for God. On the contrary, I vowed in my baptismal covenant to seek and serve Christ in all persons, I find authority in a Bible that begins with humanity being made in God's image, and I confess a Christ that was incarnated and took on flesh and bones.

My union with God is not a substitute for my own sexual expression with another person, it is the root and the anchor of it. In my painful attempts at responding to this yearning, I reacted to that deep impulse to consume beauty and sexuality and deep connection in the world by watching pornography, fantasizing about other people's bodies, obsessing for hours about sexual encounters, and often testing the boundaries of relationships with people to whom I was attracted. The union I yearn for, though, is not about breadth or options or variety. The union with God, which is the root

22. Keller, *On the Mystery*, 38.

23. Catholic Church United States Conference of Catholic Bishops, *United States Catholic Catechism for Adults*, 312.

of this yearning, is about depth, intimacy, connection, and commitment. In addiction, I was trying to have all the potentialities, all the possibilities, and grasp them all at once, make them all become actualities by myself.

I was operating out of that chaotic depth that is the depth of God in me, my union with the divine, and trying to take hold of all the potentialities of that depth at once, trying to control them, trying, like Eve, to reach out and grasp them all. All the images, all the videos, all the bodies, all the people, all the intimacies. But what I found was that the possibilities of the impossible depth of relationship were actualized when I let go and let be, when I engaged with the depth rather than attempt to control it, when I got into depth in *one* relationship. And that is different than the possibilities of *breadth* at which I had been grasping.

Some call the chaos evil. But the response to chaos is not order but engagement. It is not control but letting be. Addiction shows us how little control we have. How control doesn't work. The very thing I do not want to do I do. And this invites us to engage and gently let be rather than to continue trying to control and grasp through those addictive/sinful behaviors.

At its best, I have found that intimacy in intentional, committed relationship is the most authentic expression of this desire for the transcendent, and connects me to God, to myself, and to my partner in a way that acting out always tried to do but never could. It is this deep, sexual, instinctual desire for connection and intimacy and knowing and being known fully, in mind, body, and spirit, that I can only begin to connect with in intimate committed relationship, but that I was always trying to find in sexual acting out.

There is a deeply erotic nature to this union with God that is the root of sexuality, and we have been given bodies to connect with this erotic union in our created world, and in the midst of my acting out I was stopping at my body, only using this one dimension of myself to connect with just one dimension of the world around me. This deep erotic intimacy is not just a yearning of the body, though that is the most apparent expression of it. It is a deep erotic intimacy also of the mind and of the heart. It is a union of the entirety of our humanity, and intimacy in mind, heart, and body requires relationship, not just sexual acting out.

Thinking again about one of those Ten Commandments, idolatry is not replacing one thing with another thing, like putting a person or an idol or some physical object in place of God. It is instead seeing something that is multi-dimensional one-dimensionally, like how in sex addiction I see a person who is so complex and comprehensive and has a whole universe inside them yet fixate on just one part of who they are. I create and fixate on those images of who I think people are, who they are in my head, but never who they *actually* are at all. I fantasize about the physical appearance of a person and delete parts of them that I consider imperfect and change parts of them into some made up ideal I have of a human body or of sexuality, and in the end, they are a total illusion, completely detached from their reality.

The same thing goes for God, in that God is multi-dimensional, unknowable, undefinable; just focusing on one dimension of God and worshiping that is idolatrous. So idolatry isn't just ascribing divinity to a thing that isn't God but also seeing anything as one-dimensional rather than in its true multi-dimensional self. Reducing a subject to an object is idolatry in all its forms. Idolatry is being focused on only the image and not the likeness, only the surface and not the depth.

Tools for Our Journey

Sins are not offenses against God, they are tools used by God to reengage us, to reconnect us to our depth, which is at the same time the depth of God and the depth of inter-relationality that connects all things to one another. It is the same inter-relationality from which all potentialities, both joyful and painful, find their actuality. In missing the mark, in sinning, we disengage from relational depth and cause suffering in our connection to God, ourselves, and one another, but in and through that suffering we are invited to greater depth than we had before. The goal of our spiritual journey is not to remain sinless, the mark is not avoiding that arbitrary list of behaviors that God does not like any more than the goal of recovery from addiction is abstinence.

We are called to walk this path of our sin and suffering, recognizing them as tools for our journey and invitations back to our own depth, to one another, and to God. Our sins, our addictions, are indicative of our connection to God, not our disconnection. Our missing the mark is not evil, it is indicative of the fact that we are aimed at the transcendent, real, and divine. Sin is an invitation to share the ways we are missing the mark with one another, to communicate the truth of our suffering in relationship, and thus to share the locations of our missed arrows on the wall where the target has been. It is an invitation to deeper relationship, to plunge headlong into the chaos of our interdependence and the truth that we know nothing apart from our relationship with one another. As the anonymous author of the mystical classic *The Cloud of Unknowing* implores us, "beat on that thick cloud of unknowing with the sharp arrow of longing and never stop loving, no matter what comes your way."[24]

If addiction and sin are one and the same, and our Christian understanding of salvation and the work of Jesus is so linked to sin, how does this view of addiction affect our theology of salvation and the way we understand Jesus' work? In turn, it will also show us how we are missing the mark when it comes to our incorporation of addiction into our faith communities.

24. Butcher, *The Cloud of Unknowing*, 21–22.

6

Salvation and Addiction

I began my second year of seminary with the beginning cracks of healing covering every part of me. I was still watching pornography and I was still lying about it, both to my wife and to myself. At the same time, though, there was a softness inside that had never been there before. There was an openness inside of me. It felt like something new was under construction. In the midst of all this I reentered the seminary community, and my life has never been the same since.

There was a girl. We were in the same incoming class the year before and had become friends over the first year of school. I had a crush on her from the moment I saw her the year before and still did. I told myself that it was just like any of the other women to whom I had been attracted over the long history of my addiction. I had always jumped from one person to the next, fantasizing about them, obsessing about them, and often getting close to them without ever going so far as physical intimacy. I had always practiced some kind of physical restraint with the women I had been attracted to, channeling that energy toward internet pornography, but I was always much more willing to test the limits of emotional intimacy.

From the beginning though, this felt different. We both lived in the same apartment complex, so we began carpooling to school together. We spent a lot of time in the car going to and from school that fall, talking and sharing things about our lives. We carpooled for the whole fall and though we didn't have the same class schedule anymore entering the spring decided to continue carpooling. We just kept spending more and more time sitting around talking. We would sit in the car in the parking lot for hours sharing experiences we were having or different parts of our lives. It felt like something was awakening in me that had been lying dormant, or maybe had never been there before. It felt like it was coming from that same deep down place that I could never define before, but instead of destroying intimacy, this was helping it grow.

The only catch was, we were both married. In March of that spring semester we had a conversation naming our feeling for one another. We recognized how we were falling in love, and at the same time the unfathomable complications of that truth. We told one another we could be in love but that we could not end our marriages. We were wrong.

From that moment, my heart had the final fatal fissures to crack it open once and for all. Love was doing something in me that I had never experienced before, and once I realized that, I knew I could not live in the illusion I had been in anymore. It was the most wonderful, life-giving, terrifying, exciting, anxious, and fearful time in my life. Over the next weeks and months we continued to fall in love as my marriage fell apart and I began to lie to everyone around me in hopes of not getting in trouble. I lied to my wife, I lied to the school, I lied to my friends, and I lied to my family. I was afraid and in love and everything was falling apart. Life won. It had overcome me, it had taken me under in its overpowering rip current, and I am more thankful than I could ever express in words that it did.

My marriage fell apart. My reputation fell apart. My friendships fell apart. I fell apart. Eventually everyone found out about our relationship. My wife, the school, my friends and family, all found out. All of those structures I had built up came crashing down. We decided that it was best for both of us, though we knew we were in love, to take time away from one another. We both took a year off of school and moved back to our home states for the year. Everything was gone. All of the lies I had told myself and everyone around me for my whole life evaporated in the light of day. I found myself in Tallahassee, Florida, alone, with no friends, no family, and out of touch with my person. And it was the best thing that ever happened to me.

What Is Salvation?

We have established addiction and sin as one and the same experience, two ways of talking about the same phenomenon. Both terms are used to refer to the ways we cause suffering in our own lives by making attempts at the transcendent, and at grasping and controlling the chaos of our lives that bubbles up from our depths. They indicate our connection to these depths, to the depths of God in us, and are therefore both the source of our suffering and an invitation to engage with our own depth and chaos. Not only that, but they invite us to engage at the same time with the depth and chaos of the world, made up of the intricate web of relationship, of inter-relationship, that makes up our humanity, and that makes up God.

If addiction and sin are so inextricably linked, then addiction must in some way be connected to our theology of salvation. Most approaches to soteriology, the theology in the Christian tradition of Jesus' saving work in the world, emphasize sin as the primary target of Jesus' ministry. One such model, which in one form or another permeates the conversation about salvation, is the substitutionary atonement theory, originally proposed by Anselm of Canterbury in the eleventh century. This approach espouses the view that God sent Jesus into the world as a sacrifice to atone for the mas-sive debt built up against God by the sins of humanity, and therefore Jesus' primary mission in the world was to die, as a sacrifice, on behalf of human-ity to appease God. To many, this is what it means to say that Jesus is a "savior" and thus brought "salvation." Whether substitutionary atonement is explicitly stated or not, it has shaded the Christian narrative that human-ity has been messed up, deviated from the original plan, and Jesus is the necessary sacrifice to rescue us from certain damnation and punishment at the hands of an angry God. The fall of humanity through that original sin led to a buildup of offenses against God and thus the need for an emergency savior to settle the debt between God and humanity.

With a renewed understanding of addiction and sin, this narrative begins to shake and shift and take on a new form. Recognizing addiction as indicative of our connection to, rather than disconnection from, God, and reading sin as behavior that causes us to suffer rather than an offense against God, what are we to make of Jesus' work of salvation? In light of these approaches to addiction and sin, this classical and still widely ac-cepted narrative of salvation breaks down. What, then, are the implications of Jesus' life for our lives if it is not framed by wrath, punishment, blood sacrifice, and debt? Whatever they are, they do not imply an absence of suffering, as we have seen and experienced through this new way of under-standing addiction and sin, but a new way of understanding how suffering fits into the soteriological narrative.

Savior or Healer?

The word salvation is a translation of the Greek word *sōtēr*, from which we get the theological term soteriology. *Sōtēr*, while most often translated as "salvation," can also be translated as "preservation" or "safety." It comes from the verb *sōzō*, which means "to save" or "to rescue." These definitions are the framework within which this deeply ingrained narrative of Jesus coming to rescue a world messed up beyond repair is formed. Like all Greek words, *sōzō* carries a number of possible translations, each of which adds a unique strand to the fabric of its meaning. While often translated "to save" or "to rescue," the verb *sōzō* can also mean "to heal." When these definitions are held together, this word *sōzō* takes on a new shape, and thus begins to reshape the very narrative of salvation that Christianity has so loudly proclaimed for so long. In light of "healing," "save" and "rescue" seem to point to a different kind of action.

To save or rescue someone or something through healing indicates a different action than a swift removal of humanity from the possibility of vengeful punishment and eternal damnation at the hands of an angry God. To heal someone is not to save or rescue them from some sort of cosmic destruction, but to save or rescue them from *suffering*. Not suffering deferred to the afterlife but suffering that occurs right now. Like Richard Rohr said, "We are punished by our sins, not for our sins."[1] Punishment for our sins requires Jesus to save us from revenge by an angry God. Punishment by our sins means that Jesus came to save us *from our sins*, from our own destructive behavior, to "save" us by healing us, here and now, when our suffering is happening. This is the soteriological shift from the end of times to the present moment. Emotional or spiritual healing is a saving or rescuing from pain and suffering, not in the future, not into eternity, but here and now. There is an immediacy to this salvation, a newness, not just something that happens on a cosmic level, but on an immanently personal one.

Soteriology is not so much about how Jesus' actions in life, death, and resurrection saved us from the wrath of an angry God, or saved us from eternal damnation, but about how Jesus' actions in life, death, and resurrection *heal* us here and now. Salvation is about more than defining the way Jesus saves us, it is about defining the way Jesus *heals* us, not just Jesus' saving work in the world, but Jesus' *healing* work in the world. Any theology of salvation, any understanding of the implications of Jesus' ministry

1. Rohr, *Laughing and Weeping*.

in the world removed from healing, removed from a response to human suffering, focused solely on individual confession and heavenly assurance is not salvation. Soteriology is our theology of how Jesus heals, right here and now.

Jesus, the Pioneer

Healing, of course, does not happen overnight. It does not happen in a moment. It is not as simple as "Once you accept Jesus Christ as your Lord and Savior everything will automatically get better. Your suffering will end. You will be at peace." That is no truer than saying that once you admit you are an addict then everything will immediately be fixed. No. There is a lot of work to do. That is just the first step on a long path, a path that no one, not even Jesus, can walk for us. So, there is a balance to this work of salvation, between the one-time work of Jesus and the ongoing journey to which we are called. There is a balance between the work Jesus did on our behalf and the work we are called to do now.

If the Christian understanding of Jesus' work in the world in his life, death, and resurrection, is that he came to die for our sins, then we are missing the life and resurrection part. Not only that, but we are ignoring his words in the Gospels as to what it is he came to do. Jesus said, "Take up [your] cross and follow me" (Matt 16:24). He did not say, "Watch me take up my cross and do all the work for you." Instead, Jesus' message to his disciples was that the Son of Man (the human one) must be rejected, suffer, and die and then be raised on the third day, and that this did not just include him doing it *instead* of us, but as a "pioneer of our salvation" (Heb 2:10). He did it as one who would go ahead and embody (incarnate) the path that we are all called to take. Salvation is not about confessing Jesus as Lord and Savior, it is not about believing that Jesus *is* one thing or another, it is about believing *in* Jesus' path and following it ourselves.

A pioneer, rather than a blood sacrifice for the settlement of a debt, implies something ongoing, something that we are still called to do now. A pioneer is a leader, a founder of a path, who journeys into the unknown, discovers newness in previously uncharted territory, and blazes a trail. And for what purpose? Simply to have done it? So that no one else will ever have to walk it? No. A pioneer sets out into that unknown so that others may someday follow them. It is not an individual mission or isolated journey, it is a path that is meant to be followed, that is meant to be walked by all, not by just the first one to have walked it.

Jesus' life, death, and resurrection was not a one-time payment, but a journey that we are all called to follow him on now. A journey of suffering, rejection, death, resurrection, and new life. A journey that we will walk many times in our lives, but that leads us out of the bondage we put ourselves in. A journey that we can take with confidence or, as the writer of Hebrews implores, "run with perseverance the race that is set before us, looking to Jesus the pioneer and perfecter of our faith, who for the sake of the joy that was set before him endured the cross, disregarding its shame" (Heb 12:1).

What has happened to Jesus, if we are willing to follow this path, will happen to us. And it will not happen without suffering, it will cost us those things we think we must have. It will cost us our life, but it is our life that we will find. We can run with perseverance this race, a race that follows the path cut through the wilderness of our deepest fears and yearning, through the deepest parts of ourselves, by Jesus, the pioneer of our salvation, and for the joy set before us endure the suffering along the way. For we can know, and have experienced, that our addictions have caused us suffering, but a path has been revealed, incarnated, embodied, and it is a path to freedom, a path that no one can walk for us, but one that we can be assured God walks with us.

The Wounds That Heal

One of the verses of Scripture most commonly used to summarize the work of Jesus in the world and thus the popular view of salvation is John 3:16. "For God so loved the world that he gave his only Son, so that everyone who believes in him may not perish but may have eternal life" (John 3:16). There are many conclusions about Jesus' work in salvation that have been drawn from this single verse of Scripture. One is that salvation means saving someone from eternal death and delivering them to eternal life. The other is that this deliverance is dependent on the individual's ability to believe in Jesus. And finally, there is a clear assumption that God sent Jesus into the world to die for us.

When we focus too much on a single verse of Scripture we do ourselves a great disservice in missing the larger theological and scriptural context within which that verse lives. There is a lot going on in the Bible, including a vast array of genres all interwoven into this Book of many books. There are layers of cultural context and assumptions, both in terms of the broader societal structures the authors and individuals found themselves in and the various religious contexts within which they were located. For one, most of the writers of the various books in the New Testament were operating from a Jewish worldview, with varying degrees of familiarity with Hebrew Scripture. When we remove this verse from its larger context in the Gospel of John, we lose the nuance of what the Gospel writer is trying to convey about salvation and the work of Jesus in the world.

When we read John 3:16 with the preceding two verses, John 3:14 and 3:15, we see a very different picture of salvation painted by Jesus than what we can glean from just the 16th verse itself. Jesus says, "And just as Moses lifted up the serpent in the wilderness, so must the Son of Man be lifted up, that whoever believes in him may have eternal life. For God so loved the world that he gave his only Son, so that everyone who believes in him may not perish but may have eternal life" (John 3:14–16). In adding the context of just these two verses we are met with a dynamic interplay of meaning, implication, and depth of tradition that is far beyond a simple one-step guide to salvation. We find Jesus referencing a story from the book of Numbers in the Hebrew Scriptures in order to put his understanding of salvation and his work in the world into the context of a larger narrative of history. Jesus is using the truth of a story to indicate the truth of salvation, of the saving work he is doing in the world.

The story Jesus is referencing is from Numbers 21:1–9:

> From Mount Hor [the Israelites] set out by the way to the Red Sea, to go around the land of Edom; but the people became impatient on the way. The people spoke against God and against Moses, "Why have you brought us up out of Egypt to die in the wilderness? For there is no food and no water, and we detest this miserable food." Then the LORD sent poisonous serpents among the people, and they bit the people, so that many Israelites died. The people came to Moses and said, "We have sinned by speaking against the LORD and against you; pray to the LORD to take away the serpents from us." So Moses prayed for the people. And the LORD said to Moses, "Make a poisonous serpent, and set it on a pole; and everyone who is bitten shall look at it and live." So Moses made a serpent of bronze, and put it upon a pole; and whenever a serpent bit someone, that person would look at the serpent of bronze and live.

Israel is the ultimate addict. When faced with the discomfort of transition, of the desert, of the place in between leaving suffering and entering the promised land, they consistently want to return to that which does not work, to bondage and slavery, and to the suffering they know rather than the promise of what might be but is not yet. Sobriety sucks. It feels like death. It is a desert wasteland where you have not yet figured out how to live without your addictive behavior and each occurrence of not partaking in that behavior feels like a punch in the gut. The voice in your head calls out: why did we leave that (drink, porn, drug, etc.) just to wither up and die out here in the unknown? Sobriety—the first moments of engaging with the wandering chaos of the desert land that lies immediately outside the bondage of addiction—is enough to make you wish for the addiction again, no matter how painful it was.

Jesus is using this story as a metaphor for the spiritual journey he is inviting everyone to follow. The Israelites cry out to God to remove the snakes and take the source of their suffering away. But God does no such thing. Instead of removing the snakes that God sent, God tells Moses to make a snake out of bronze and put it on a pole so that whoever is bitten by a snake shall look at it and live. Rather than *removing* the source of suffering, God *transforms* the source of suffering into a source of healing. The snakes are still there, the consequences must be lived with, but God responds to the suffering with a source of healing, that again is not the removal of the suffering, but the healing of it through its very source. By lifting up the serpent on a pole, gazing at it directly, in full view, in the full light of day, in front of everyone, lifting it up in vulnerability, the person is healed.

And thus, Jesus says, it will be with him. There is more to this journey of believing than just professing Jesus as Lord and Savior. Jesus ties this story directly to what is happening in his life, death, and resurrection. Belief here means more than just signing on to a specific tenet of doctrine about who Jesus is or is not. It is about having enough faith in Jesus, believing in him enough, trusting him enough, to walk this journey that he has set before us. One that clearly includes suffering, uses our very sources of suffering to destroy us, but then uses those same sources of suffering to transform us, to bring us to new life, to bring us back to ourselves, to help us engage with the world and ourselves and God in a new way. It puts us back in touch with our own depths, which are the same as the depths of God.

Jesus would die on the cross from wounds in his side and hands, but these very wounds were to become sources of healing and salvation for the whole world. We may be afraid of our addictions, our capacity to cause suffering, and the chaos in us and around us, but Jesus sets before us a path not of fear but of joy. Rather than hiding our addictions and wanting to cut out and remove those parts of ourselves that we don't like, we are called to raise them up high in the light of day, gaze at them, and let them gaze back at us. In doing this we let ourselves be transformed and let those very sources of suffering be transformed in us.

As we see in the resurrected Jesus, those wounds are not healed, at least not in the way we think of healing. Even healing itself has taken on a new shape in Jesus' saving work. Healing no longer means to close up a wound, to cover up those places of suffering. Healing is the transforming of wounds into sources of healing, where we can touch the very places where we have been destroyed and find hope. Healing is not the removal of suffering, healing is the transformation of suffering for the sake of our own transformation and the transformation of the world. It is a transformation we can bring about when we allow ourselves to die, to be brought to new life, and to engage deeply with ourselves and the world, through our wounds, the sources of our powerless power. Addiction is not a threat to the world, it is our gift to the world, and a gift we all possess.

The Narrow Path

In the Gospel of Matthew, Jesus addresses this lifelong journey in another way, saying, "Enter through the narrow gate; for the gate is wide and the road is easy that leads to destruction, and there are many who take it. For the gate is narrow and the road is hard that leads to life, and there are few who find it" (Matt 7:13–14). This word "path" is the same Greek word that is sometimes translated as "way," as it is in John's Gospel when Jesus says, "I am the *way*, and the truth, and the life" (John 14:6). To say that the way is narrow and hear that Jesus is the way has in the past led some to assert that Jesus is talking again here about the necessity of confessing belief as a prerequisite for salvation. This is not the picture Jesus is painting though. Jesus, the pioneer, is pointing to a journey, not a one-time statement of belief. He is pointing to the lived experience of walking a path, moving through a gate, and following him on the way, which he incarnates and embodies. "I *am* the way, the truth, the life" means "I am the embodiment of a journey that you must walk."

The path and gate that lead to life are small and narrow not because the journey is specific to Jesus or to belief in one person or doctrine, but because the path is specific to you and to every person. The path is only as wide as your foot because only you can walk it. The gate is only as wide as your addiction, and Jesus is calling you to pass through it to new life. This is a path that develops and unfolds only as you walk it. The gate is wide and the road easy that leads to destruction, which is the necessary beginning of our journey, where we are living out of our false self, disengaged from our depths, from our union with God, believing that we are in control, that there are limitless options, a width and breadth of possibilities all of which we can bring to actualization through our own control. Living in the midst of our addictive behavior, our sins, is the easy path, the wide gate, that leads to suffering. But this path is not a separate path from the narrow one.

Our suffering slowly chips away at the width of the path as we continue on our journey. It gets narrower and narrower as the pain of our addictions invites us to engage ultimately on the narrow path and through the narrow gate that leads to life. It is just that, though—an invitation. It is not a journey that is forced on us. If we want, we can stand at the precipice of this narrow path, able to make out the shape of that narrow gate off in the distance, while we sit in our suffering, addictions, and sins. God is there with us also. But every painful experience, every addictive act, every sin is a new invitation to keep walking.

We are invited to follow Jesus through that narrow gate and engage with our chaos, our addictions, and our suffering. We are called to follow him even to death, to take up our cross, be crucified in vulnerability and powerlessness, and enter into new life, where suffering is transformed into healing. Thus, part of our journey is learning what our cross is to take up. Like the serpent in the wilderness, we must identify the source of our suffering in order to lift it up and transform it into a source of healing. As Teresa of Avila wrote, "[God] is pleased to treat you like people who are strong and give you a cross to bear on earth like that which his majesty himself also bore. What better sign of a friendship is there than for [God] to give what he gave himself."[2] Like Jesus, we are each given a cross, which Jesus invites us to take up and follow him. This cross is our addiction, a built-in invitation, born out of our connection to God and to the depth of God in us.

2. Teresa, *The Way of Perfection*, 127.

A Struggle with God

As noted earlier, from the words of Catherine Keller, "If the honest struggle with oneself that Paul recommends is engaged, the weakness that shames us can become a laboratory in a new kind of power. Our worst vulnerability can become, rather than a site of personal disillusion, the opening into an illimitable interactivity." This struggle is what I am talking about when I say engagement. We often speak of a person who identifies as an addict as someone who is struggling with addiction. This can make this engagement with addiction feel oppositional, like a person fighting with a demon or with an enemy. This is not the struggle referenced above, and this is not the struggle of engagement to which we are invited through addiction.

The struggle of addiction is less like a fight with an enemy and more like the struggle between Jacob and God in the book of Genesis. Jacob, on his way to make amends with his brother Esau, having deceived him and stolen his inheritance many years before and having since been deceived and suffered himself, sends his family and community away so he can be alone on the night before he is to meet with Esau, afraid of his brother's wrath. Having sent all of his possessions and everything he had across the river he had this interaction:

> Jacob was left alone; and a man wrestled with him until daybreak. When the man saw that he did not prevail against Jacob, he struck him on the hip socket; and Jacob's hip was put out of joint as he wrestled with him. Then he said, "Let me go, for the day is breaking." But Jacob said, "I will not let you go, unless you bless me." So he said to him, "What is your name?" And he said, "Jacob." Then the man said, "You shall no longer be called Jacob, but Israel, for you have striven with God and with humans, and have prevailed." Then Jacob asked him, "Please tell me your name." But he said, "Why is it that you ask my name?" And there he blessed him. So Jacob called the place Peniel, saying, "For I have seen God face to face, and yet my life is preserved." The sun rose upon him as he passed Penuel, limping because of his hip. (Gen 32:24–31)

As we see in this story, it is almost impossible in the midst of this struggle to recognize that it is God with whom we are grappling. It is not until afterwards that Jacob recognizes that it was God he was wrestling. Up until that final interaction, it seemed like just another man, an enemy; in the dark of night, in the loneliness of solitude and fear, it appeared as an opponent to fight and destroy. But this struggle, in the dawning of a new day, showed itself to be holy. Not without fear and suffering, not without wounding. But holy nonetheless. The outcome was not that Jacob walked away perfectly healthy and unaffected. Much to the contrary, Jacob was wounded, but in this struggle, in this engagement with the source of his suffering, his identity is revealed to him: "You shall no longer be called Jacob, but Israel" (Gen 32:29), a name that literally means God (*'el*) fights (*sārah*). Not only is Jacob's true self revealed through this struggle, but it is the struggle itself which has become part of his identity as one who "struggled" with God. He is wounded, but with a deeper identity, carrying that wound into the world for healing, forgiveness, compassion and prosperity. He goes from here to embrace his brother, and to bring forth a great nation that will bear his name, and come into contact with its own suffering in the desert.

In Jacob we see what it means to engage with our addictions. We think at first that we are fighting for our lives, or struggling with something evil. In the fear and sorrow of this dark night, of rock bottom, we can't image that anything good can come of this. But if we are able, if the grace of God brings us somehow to the dawn, we recognize that our struggle was not getting in the way of God, our struggle was with God. Our struggle emerged from the depth of God in ourselves, our union with the divine. We recognize that the source of our suffering is that very depth, the yearning that comes from our connection with the divine, and that our path to healing, to wholeness, is not away from that suffering, but *through* it. We will limp away from this struggle, having come face to face with God, with ourselves, and with God in us. We will see that, in all its messiness, in all its fear, in all its suffering, somehow, the grace of God is not just in the recovery, but in the fall itself. As fourteenth-century Christian mystic Julian of Norwich wrote, "we first fall and then we see it; and both are from the mercy of God."[3]

If salvation is based on the cross and the cross is based on the golden serpent, then salvation is about being healed through engagement with our sources of greatest suffering and allowing them to be transformed into sources of healing. Addiction is our invitation to admit that we are causing suffering, to lift this realization up, gaze at it, and let it transform us and open our wounds, so they can be sources of healing for ourselves, others, and the world around us. Jesus showed us that the healing of wounds is not about closing them up or covering them, but about leaving them open, transforming them into places where people can explore, find healing

3. Julian, *Showings*, 300.

themselves, and find God. It is having a part of our selves that we believed to be evil recognized as being good. It is the transformation of a place of suffering into healing, because it has been redeemed, or reclaimed, by God and by us. With this understanding in mind, what does the church have to offer the world, first in the sacraments and then in community?

7

Addiction and the Sacraments

*It wasn't until my life had fallen apart that twelve-step programs for sex ad-
diction and the possibility of calling myself an addict even made it onto my
radar. It was August 2014 and I found myself alone, in a basement apartment in Tallahassee, Florida, a place where I knew no one, in the middle of
a divorce and far removed from the only person I so desperately wanted to be
with. I was lonely, broke, and utterly unsure of my personal and vocational
future. All of life was up in the air, and I felt for the first time how utterly out
of control it all really was. Lying on the floor of that basement apartment that
first night there, I felt rock bottom for the first time. All of the scratching and
clawing and lying and manipulating—it had all led to this.*

*As painful as it was, there was also a newfound sense of inner depth. It
felt like a dark hope that now resided in the same place that I had always felt
my compulsion to act out. There was this dark, quiet spaciousness right in the
middle of me, as if a large mass made up of years of addictive behavior, painful relationships, lies, and fears had suddenly been transformed into a pool
of luminescent darkness. The chasm that had been carved out over so many
years of destructive behavior was now full of emptiness. It didn't feel like these
painful things had suddenly vanished or been removed from me. Instead, it
felt like they had been used to make this unbelievable spaciousness inside me
and transformed into the raw material of hope. There was now a depth that
had been there all along but that I had spent my life avoiding, suppressing,
and controlling. And in so doing I had been controlled. Somehow this depth
was holding me gently, not controlling me, but just letting me be. It was carrying me through this time of fear, pain, and desperation.*

In this newly opened space inside I could feel a new openness to everything. My efforts to control had failed time and time again and had brought me to the stark realization that I was not in control. But I was not being controlled either. I was being invited to a new engagement with myself and with the world around me. All of the ideas of God that had helped me feel in control, and all of my certainties about myself and my faith were gone. They had been stripped away, crumbling with the rest of me. Instead of feeling hopeless and fearful, though, I felt an openness to everything. It was a humility that could only be born out of humiliation, out of being forced to come face to face with my humanity.

As I began this year away, this spiritual confluence helped me begin to engage with my own spirituality for the first time. It helped me question the assumptions I had about myself, my vocation, and God. I was open to engaging with spirituality for the first time and faced with the reality of that chasm and my lifelong intellectualizing of my experience and faith. In that time, I had a mentor who invited me to my first twelve-step meeting. I began to share openly about my addiction to pornography, and I found that every time I spoke openly about it something in me was transformed. It felt like a new kind of power that was only born through admitting powerlessness. I started a spiritual practice of daily contemplative prayer, sitting in intentional silence each day and facing head-on the chaos inside me. But this chaos was no longer the same as inner turmoil. It was not the chaos I had created outside of me by trying to overpower and control the chaos inside.

Instead, when I became silent and allowed myself to become aware of the depths churning in me, that chaos began to cultivate in me new possibilities. My whole addicted life I had tried to grasp those possibilities, but now they produced things in me that I never could have dreamed for myself. This is not to say that everything became perfect and peaceful all of a sudden. To the contrary, I was still scared, anxious, and unsure, but somehow, I had an ability to sit with it instead of hating it. I felt a growing capacity to befriend this chaos which now seemed capable of leading to life, instead of more destruction. It was the hardest, scariest, most anxious year of my life, and the most blessed time I have known.

Invited to Practice

One of the reasons the twelve steps are so effective is because they are practical. They involve a clear step-by-step guide and specific practices as markers on the journey of recovery. As we have seen, the intertwining and reconnection of addiction and sin brings addiction back into the fold of a Christian theology of theological anthropology, sin, and salvation, as well as Christian social ethics and moral theology. To look at it from a process perspective like that of Catherine Keller, in observing this unfolding of addiction we have witnessed its coinciding enfolding into the multilayered complexity of the Christian tradition, and thus into its theology. This Christian theology, though, also has a practical, practice-oriented side to it, much like the twelve steps. While different parts of the Christian tradition vary widely in their worship styles, falling somewhere on a broad spectrum of liturgical styles, and in the number of such communal practices with which they engage, there are two that are held across almost all of them. These two sacred communal practices are the sacraments of baptism and Eucharist.

Over the long theological history of the Christian tradition, the understanding and belief surrounding these two sacraments has varied widely, constantly being interpreted and reinterpreted, read in light of new theological developments, and often finding itself the cause of schism in the life of the church. Today, as many different denominations as there are in Christianity, there as many different interpretations of what goes on during the sacred rites of baptism and Eucharist. As we transition from a theological exploration of addiction and its implications for other parts of theology, we now begin to explore what a theologically informed response to addiction looks like in a Christian context, both from the perspective of those within a church community and those unaffiliated. As a community founded on the life of a person solely interested in being in communion with sinners, the church has as part of its very DNA the tools and ability to engage deeply with suffering, sin, and addiction.

Addiction is an invitation to pause and recognize what is not working in our lives. Even more than that, it is an indication that we are yearning for true union with God, with the transcendent and eternal, and yet missing the mark. In coming to terms with this reality we are invited into the slow work of engaging with the chaos within us, looking at those hard truths inside, and opening up to God's grace and transformation. In all four of the Gospels Jesus refers to this process of dying to the way we have been in order to find new life, saying "Those who find their life will lose it, and those who lose their life for my sake will find it" (Matt 10:39). Jesus goes on to model this very process in his death and resurrection, and consistently exhorts those around him to "follow ." In his death and resurrection Jesus models with his own life that dying is not the end of anything, but rather the transformation into something new.

This is in many ways the work of the twelve steps. When done intentionally, they are a step-by-step guide to dying to the ways we have been in our lives and to being transformed and healed. They are about admitting powerlessness, admitting fault, admitting resentment, taking inventory, emptying the self, confessing, coming into closer union with God, and experiencing a spiritual awakening. The twelve steps are not intended to just lead to sobriety; they are intended to lead to a *spiritual awakening*. They are meant to bring us face to face with what is not working, to create a space for us to share how addiction is hurting us, and then to do the painful work of slowly dying to the ways of that addictive behavior.

In the same way, when rightly understood, this is the intention behind the sacraments. This is what Jesus is calling us to do when he asks us to "follow" him. It is to take very seriously the fact that we have to die, and that this death will lead to new life. This is the work the twelve steps are undertaking within the process of addiction and recovery, but this is also our call as a community meant to follow Christ in our own spiritual recovery from sin and addiction. It is a truly painful death first to admit the ways in which we are missing the mark in our lives, then to actually go through the process of admitting powerlessness over those behaviors and asking God to transform these yearnings through death. This, though, is the promise of the resurrection. As Jesus shows us, to die to addictive behavior, or to sin, is not to have it removed. Death does not mean the end of something. Rather, death means the transformation of death into life, the transformation of wounds into places of healing, the transformation of sins into virtues, and the transformation of separation into union.

The Sacraments

At the deepest level, the sacraments of the Christian tradition are meant to bring us into deeper union with ourselves, with one another, and with God. They each present a unique entryway into doing this work of dying to ourselves and being transformed into new life. The two major sacraments are baptism and Eucharist, while the five other sacramental rites are confirmation, marriage, ordination, unction, and confession. These sacraments are markers along our lifelong spiritual journey of dying to ourselves and our addictions and being transformed and healed through God's grace as we continue to take part in following Jesus to death and resurrection. As the Book of Common Prayer defines them, in the catechetical section entitled "An Outline of the Faith," sacraments are most basically "outward and visible signs of inward and spiritual grace, given by Christ as sure and certain means by which we receive that grace."[1]

There is a delicate balance to be found between the "outward and visible sign" and the "inward and spiritual grace" of the sacraments. We do nothing to earn this grace of God that works through us to transform and heal us, but we do take part in opening to that grace. The grace of God is moving no matter what we do. It breaks into our lives, moves us, changes us, transforms us, and sustains us. And yet we recognize that there is something that we do to take part in this grace. It is the same for the twelve steps, or any kind of spiritual practice. The point is not the practice itself, it is what God is doing in the midst of the practice. Yet it is still somehow ours to enter into, and at the same time God's to bring us into.

Therefore the sacraments can, like the steps, be markers for us on the journey toward transformation, healing, and union. They can all be reminders to us that death is not the end of life, but the beginning of it, and therefore that we are invited into death, over and over again, to be transformed and healed through it. Addiction and sin are not things that are bad or evil that need to be removed. To die to sin, or to die to addiction, is not to have them washed away by God, but rather washed through and transformed into something else. As the Bible, the Gospels, Jesus' death and resurrection, and all of creation show us, death is not what we think. There is no such thing as an end, there is only transformation and new life.

Baptized and Buried

This new life is the promise of baptism. As Paul writes, "Do you not know that all of us who have been baptized into Christ Jesus were baptized into his death? Therefore, we have been buried with him by baptism into death, so that, just as Christ was raised from the dead by the glory of the Father, so we too might walk in newness of life" (Rom 6:3–4). Paul is reminding us that baptism is not meant to be a sign of membership, but a sign of death and resurrection. The Greek word for baptism means "dipping" or "immersion." Baptism is meant to be a full bodily immersion into water. It is meant

1. Episcopal Church, The Book of Common Prayer, 857.

to show the death and resurrection that is inherent in the lifelong spiritual journey.

This is the understanding that former Archbishop of Canterbury Rowan Williams is trying to call us back to in his book *Being Christian: Baptism, Bible, Eucharist, Prayer*. Williams asserts that "baptism means being with Jesus 'in the depths': the depths of human need, including the depths of our own selves in their need—but also in the depths of God's love; in the depths where the Spirit is re-creating and refreshing human life as God meant it to be."[2] This is an approach to baptism that takes seriously the necessary path of death and resurrection. Baptism is not just a one-time initiation rite into a "saved" community. Baptism is the invitation to over and over again dive into the chaos of what is swirling within us, knowing surely that we will die in the process, but that Jesus is with us in that death, and in the rising to transformed life afterwards.

This does not negate the pain of death. These deaths that we will die will certainly feel like death. They will hurt in every way that death hurts. There will be the necessary vulnerability and utter nakedness of pain and torture that Jesus displayed for us on the cross, but this is the only way to die. The path towards resurrection requires full vulnerability and a willingness to look honestly at ourselves and at the things we're doing that aren't working for us, then speaking them out in truth. This will feel like death, as vulnerability and truth telling often do. Yet, in this pain we see Jesus, who has gone before us, and modeled the truth of what it means to follow him, to march over and over toward certain death, and even more certain healing, transformation, and life. This is the promise that we can continually return to in baptism. This is the path that we are initiated into when we are baptized. This is the path to greater union with our true selves, with our neighbors, and with God. This is a union that can only happen when we take our own death and resurrection seriously. It can only happen when we die to the ways we think we are doing it right (when in fact we are only hurting ourselves in the process).

Baptism is not an initiation rite into a club, into eternal salvation, or a specific community. It is an entry into the path of descent, of engagement with chaos. As Williams goes on to say, "if we ask the question, 'Where might you expect to find the baptized?' one answer is, 'In the neighborhood of chaos' . . . . [I]n the neighborhood of Jesus—but Jesus is found in

2. Williams, *Being Christian*, 5.

the neighborhood of human confusion and suffering."[3] He adds later "you might also expect the baptized Christian to be somewhere near, somewhere in touch with, the chaos in his or her own life—because all of us live not just with chaos outside ourselves but with quite a lot of inhumanity and muddle inside us."[4] Again, we see this chaotic depth at play, calling us back to engagement. Baptism is the recognition of that calling, both to an engagement with the chaos in ourselves and in the world.

In the Episcopal church's Book of Common Prayer, there is a prayer over the water of the baptismal font that begins the rite of baptism. Look where it begins:

> We thank you, Almighty God, for the gift of water. Over it the Holy Spirit moved in the beginning of creation. Through it you led the children of Israel out of their bondage in Egypt into the land of promise. In it your Son Jesus received the baptism of John and was anointed by the Holy Spirit as the Messiah, the Christ, to lead us, through his death and resurrection, from the bondage of sin into everlasting life.[5]

We find ourselves back in the beginning, with the Holy Spirit moving over that chaotic depth of creation, the source of potential for all outcomes, in gratitude for the ways God has moved "over," "through," and "in" it. The prayer begins in the beginning and ends with "the Christ," the spiritual journey that Jesus embodied, the narrow path that leads to "everlasting life," or, as Jesus often referred to it, the kingdom of heaven. This life is everlasting and eternal, yet not in the sense that it contains infinite time into the future, but in the sense that is contains *infinite depth now*. It is indicative of the infinite depth and newness of the kingdom of heaven now, not the then-ness of it. This everlasting life is not so much about living forever but about *living infinitely now*. "The infinite *is* the enfolding of all finitudes, it *is* (in this perspective) the *complicans*, the com-pli-cating itself. And the complicating means a folding together of all in all."[6] The infinite now is an engagement with the infinite entanglement of all things, of all actualized potentialities. An engagement we are called back to by our addictions, by our sins, which are transformed through our baptism as those chaotic waters equip us to engage with that suffering over and over again.

3. Williams, *Being Christian*, 4.

4. Williams, *Being Christian*, 5.

5. Episcopal Church, The Book of Common Prayer, 306.

6. Keller, *Cloud of the Impossible*, 113.

Why do we have infant baptism? Because this journey begins the moment we are born, and we wait to recognize its unfolding to the detriment of ourselves. Just look again at the story of Adam and Eve. That chaos, that suffering, that engagement is there from the moment we are born. Have you heard the wailing cry of an infant? The deep, guttural, primal sounds of fear, of hunger, or desperation. We may grow up, we may learn, we may become rich, we may create coping mechanisms to deal with our pain, but that cry is still inside of us. It may change shape as we get older, it may change its pitch and timber, but it is still there, calling to us, calling us back to engage with it, calling us back to gaze upon it as it gazes upon us.

It calls to us from the deep, the depth calls to our depth, deep calls to deep, the deep pool of chaos, of possibility, of unknown, of uncertainty, of fear and doubt, of love and joy, of distress and retribution. From this well, this cosmic darkness, this void, God calls to us, invites us back to recognize our union, back to gentleness and compassion. That chaotic of creation still resides in us, and the waters of baptism serve as a reminder, an "outward and visible sign" of that "inward and spiritual grace." A grace that is not just the healing of wounds, but the cause of wounds and the wounds themselves. The fall and the rise from the fall. The suffering, the death, and the life. It all swirls together in those baptismal, chaotic waters, forming the possibilities of our lives, the possibilities for both joy and suffering.

Whether you use a font, or a sea shell, or the ocean or a lake or a tank of water, the waters of baptism are not for cleansing. They are not for the washing away of sin. They are not calm, peaceful waters that someone enters to step finally into a life of purity and calm peacefulness. They are the waters of chaos. They are a burial ground. They are death. They are not the way to purify ourselves of our sufferings, of our sins, of our addictions, of the ways we have hurt ourselves and other, nor are they a place of instant transformation, a promise that we will never hurt ourselves or another person again. They are not a means of getting away from our suffering, they *are* our suffering. It is not as if we are being dunked into a tank of oxyclean. It is like we are being drowned in a pool of our deepest fear, pain, sin, and addiction. It is an immersion into the parts of ourselves we would like to forget. It is a promise that we are going to be buried, we are going to die, and that we can engage with that swirling chaotic pool and know that through that suffering, through that fear and anxiety, we will be raised to new life.

We will be able to dive deep and come out the other side transformed. Not washed clean but washed through, having had every part of ourselves baptized, every piece of our lives and experiences transformed into a tool for the healing of the world. And in this we recognize that we are on the pathway to peace, a peace that is not devoid of conflict or suffering, but a peace that exists in the midst of conflict and suffering. We engage in a baptism for the forgiveness of sins, a forgiveness that is not the washing away of sin, not the removal of sin, not the expunging of a record like it never happened, but a forgiveness that is the transformation of our sources of suffering into sources of healing.

You Are What You Eat

This is the promise of all the sacraments. The other major sacrament in the Episcopal Church is the Eucharist, the sharing in communion of the body and blood of Christ, which Jesus instituted the night before he died. This meal that we partake in together is a remembrance that Christ died for us, and for many. It is a remembrance of the mystery of Jesus' death and resurrection. It is a recurring reminder of Jesus' resurrection, the saving work of that resurrection and the promise that there is no death, only transformation. And it is this transformation upon which we feast. We consume the death and resurrection of Jesus to fully embody that death and resurrection in our own lives. This is the sign of the spiritual food that sustains us on this journey of letting go, admitting powerlessness, and dying to the self and the painful behaviors of life. This is a continual reminder on our journey that what it means to follow Jesus in death and resurrection is not impossible, but also that we cannot do it alone. We can only do it with God. We consume death and resurrection to take part in death and resurrection and are brought into deeper union with God as we recognize that we are not able to do it alone, humbled in the powerful mystery that is Jesus' transformation of death into life.

As Augustine once said about the Eucharist, "it is your own mystery that is placed on the Lord's table! It is your own mystery that you are receiving!" (Sermon 272). As the waters of baptism are not some sort of magical healing fluid, the bread and wine of the Eucharist are not magical salvation food. They are a mystery. They are a mystery in the same way that it is a mystery how we heal, how wounds become healing itself, how chaos brings peace, how death brings life. The mystery is that somehow, in this communal remembrance of the death and resurrection of Jesus, the Christ, who is our journey, is really made present in the bread and wine. "It is your own mystery that is placed on the Lord's table! It is your own mystery that you are receiving." That which is already present in you, that which *dwells in you*, is what is laid on that altar before you, and is that on which you are feasting.

We consume this Christ mystery and in doing so recognize that this journey of death and resurrection, which we consume, is already really present in us, it is already unfolding in us. It is an invitation to reengage with this journey that is always there, always happening. It, like our baptism, is an invitation to engage, in mystery and humility, in compassion and gentleness, with that chaos, with that depth, in us. It is our invitation to gaze at that golden serpent, to look at and receive back the "mystery that is placed on the Lord's table," the mystery that is our own, that is Christ in us, that is death and resurrection, that is addiction and recovery, and is sin and salvation.

Markers on the Journey

Within the Christian tradition there are five other historical rites that find varying degrees of acceptance across denominations. Some understand them to be sacraments in the same way that baptism and Eucharist are understood. Some refer to them as "sacramental rites," making a distinction between the two great sacraments instituted by Jesus in the Gospels and the five other rites that developed over the course of history within the church. Some see them as significant rites of passage and markers in life, but without the need to distinguish them as in any way sacramental. These five rites are confirmation, marriage, ordination, unction or anointing at the time of death, and confession or the rite of reconciliation. Following from the two sacraments of baptism and Eucharist, these other five rites find their place in the lives of individuals and communities as markers on our spiritual journey. Each one in its own way is a reminder of this path of descent, of our invitation to engage with chaos in ourselves and in the world, that divine chaos from which springs forth all kinds of newness. Each rite has built into it an invitation back to ourselves, back to our union with God, and back to engagement with suffering and is thus a constant reminder of the tools available to Christianity on the road of transformation. They are the pit stops on the journey down the narrow path.

You will see that they line up with the crucial points of inflexion throughout our lives, those moments where we are experiencing great transition or upheaval. While each brings its own suffering and grieving, it also bears with it that potential for transformation, as that suffering continues to offer itself again and again as a source of healing for ourselves and for the world. Confirmation is a recognition and renewal of the faith into which we were baptized as infants in traditions where infant baptism is practiced. It is a declaration, an ownership, of one's faith in the mystery of Christ and the tradition of the church at a time, often in the teenage years, of great transitions in body, mind, and spirit. It is a time where we are searching for an identity, moving beyond childhood into the desert of puberty and transition to adulthood, a great already and not yet of maturation. In this time of grieving, suffering, and searching, confirmation offers the invitation to claim that we are part of something bigger than ourselves and that our identity is situated within a grander narrative than just our own. This is a recognition made on our behalf at baptism and one in which we are invited to recognize ourselves in awareness of that suffering and chaos that we have now experienced first hand.

Marriage is not just about a combining of assets or a promise of a life-long union. It is a dying to the way we have been as a single person in this world and recognizing a new commitment to another. Marriage is a death of the self, a death of the small self, and a transformation into a new life where we are giving ourselves to another in vulnerability and love. Ordination—the rite by which someone is made a deacon, priest (pastor/elder), or bishop—is similarly not a raising up to a higher status of one individual to lead many. Rather, it is a lowering down in humility to faithful servanthood and service to others. The further up the church hierarchy one goes, the greater humility that person should have in their ordination to such positions. To be ordained is not to be free to rule over more people, but to be even more restricted in what one can and cannot do in ministry. It is a very high calling, one that should be entered into with great humility, and one that should humble daily the person that is ordained.

Confession is one of the most powerful tools we have on the journey of transformation from addiction and sin. Often, we view confession as something people do when they are feeling guilty or have done something wrong. Many see it as something you do in order to receive penitential instructions from a priest. At its core, though, confession in the Christian tradition is the sacrament of emptying. This is how we empty ourselves. This is the point where we shine light on all those things that have been causing us pain. This is the fifth step of AA: "We admitted to God, to ourselves and to another person the exact nature of our wrongs."[7] This is what we do when we examine ourselves and realize that our addictions are not working. We look at all the ways we are behaving that hurt us, all of our sins, and we admit them to "God, to ourselves, and to another person."

While it is important to seek council from our spiritual leaders in our individual communities, this is not where confession should start and stop. It is something that we can utilize more than just when we are feeling guilty and more than just within the context of a reconciliation rite. One of the most powerful parts of a twelve-step meeting is the honesty and truth with which people speak about their pain, about their addictions, and about what is not working in their lives. Something transformative and healing happens when you can sit with people who are coming together for the same reason and tell your story. Even more, healing happens when you hear someone else share a story that has so much of your own in it. The power is in the community. It is in the relationships. But it is in relationships and community built around the common spiritual journey and sharing about life's deaths and resurrections in vulnerability and truth. In a similar way, the sacrament of unction is a humbling experience to ask for help and healing, even when we are asking God. This is to truly admit that we are powerless over the aging and changing of our own bodies and the chaos therein. To call on God to restore us to health and wholeness is the greatest act of union, love, trust, and humility.

Addiction, the Eight Sacrament

If a sacrament is an outward and visible sign of an inward and spiritual grace, and if we know that the grace of God is not only present in the process of recovery but in that of addiction as well, can't we say that addiction is itself a sacrament? Addictive behaviors are the outward and visible sign of an inward and spiritual grace—God's constant invitation, manifest in this yearning from our depths, back to a recognition of our depth and union with God. Just as the outward and visible sign of baptism is a plunging into the burial ground of chaos, a sign of suffering and death, so is the visible sign of addiction one of suffering. It, like baptism, Eucharist, and the other sacramental rites, is an invitation to engage with chaos, and this is the inward and spiritual grace. The grace is the fact that addiction is an invitation to reengage with our chaos and the chaos of the world, to let go

7. *Twelve Steps and Twelve Traditions*, 55.

and let be, and to recover our own depth, which is the depth of God in us. It is the same invitation, the same grace, as baptism and Eucharist. It is visible in suffering, like the death visible in baptism and Eucharist, and its grace is recovery and new life, as is present in baptism and the Eucharist.

As the baptism rite reminds us, the Spirit of God moved over the face of the deep, the infinite depth of possibility and potential. The Spirit of God never stopped moving over that chaos, what we now in the Christian tradition call the indwelling Holy Spirit hovering over the face of our chaotic depths; the depth in us that, when we try to control its outcomes and potentialities, leads to suffering, but is at the same time calling us from our depths to our depths, to reengage and return. We are called to engage with and walk this journey of life, suffering, death, and resurrection, which is a journey that happens over and over throughout our lives. It is a constant loop, the soundtrack of our lives. It is a loop that does not take place simply on the surface. It is a loop that is not a repeat of the same ground over and over, but a loop with depth, a downward spiral, with the same markers on the journey, but always at different levels of the deep. It is a journey of descent, down into the depths of ourselves, into the depths of God in us, where we find our identity, where we find our healing, where we find one another, where we find ourselves.

Waters of Recreation

We are beginning to see that the church has more ways to respond to addiction than to just feel pity and offer prayers for those who are affected. The church can recognize, in examining what it means by addiction, that we are all addicts just as we are all sinners. Then, from a place of recognizing the common journey of suffering and transformation through suffering that we are all on, we can look at the tools available in the Christian tradition and embody in the outward and visible signs of the sacraments that inward and spiritual grace that we witness to be at work in that journey. That is not the end though. There is one more offering to explore, because as we see in the Gospels, another part of Jesus ministry and journey, beyond just his death and resurrection, was about gathering people. It was the sacred act of being in community, and the healing that takes place therein. The church was built on this "Jesus movement," the movement of Jesus within community, gathering not those who believed they had it all together, but those deeply aware of their own suffering.

The church can be a place where people come because they are hurting and in pain and find not people who have all the answers but people who have all the same questions and are walking the same journey. We all have pain in our lives. We all miss the mark. So why can't we talk about it? It is our time to reclaim our own part in the healing and transformation of addiction. It happens in small groups of people, sharing with each other about their pain and joy, and doing it within a sacramental and liturgical tradition where there is liturgy and tradition to frame our journey together. There is great promise and benefit in being part of such a strong liturgical and sacramental tradition, but there is also a drawback. Far too often we make liturgy and sacraments the ends in themselves.

Liturgy and worship should be the last thing we do as a community, not the first. We too often rely on good liturgy as the means to transformation and growth. This is backwards. Liturgy should be done well, intentionally and prayerfully, but also should be a sign of the transformation and growth that is happening, not the means for that growth. In the same way, the sacraments are not ends in themselves. They are parts of a greater journey. They are symbols of a greater transformation and healing that is taking place. Liturgy and sacraments were made for the people, not the people for the liturgy and sacraments. These parts of the Christian tradition are vastly important, but transformation and healing are our roots. Sitting with one another in open conversation about sin and pain are our roots. Deaths to self in vulnerability and nakedness are our roots, and we are being called back there. The question is whether we will respond or not.

We have the resources to do it though. We have a beautiful liturgical and sacramental tradition. We have loving and prayerful theology. We are built on a solid foundation, and yet there is something more to do. There is more room to grow. There are more models to consider and incorporate, like the small-group model of the twelve steps for example. What might it look like to have small groups in our wider parish communities built to talk about addiction and sin in a liturgical and sacramental context? The twelve-step meetings are founded on ritual action and common language, but this is also our foundation and has been for our entire history.

We are built to do this, to grow and transform and heal in community. We are built to do something like small groups framed in liturgy and based on openly talking about the pains and joys of our lives; in openness; in honesty; in truth; in love; in Christ. We can be the respite for those who find themselves powerless to the behaviors that hurt them, powerless to sin and addiction. We can be a place where people come not because the liturgy is great or because the outreach committee has so many promising ideas, but because it works and there is healing happening here. We can sit down together and talk about the most painful things, because Jesus has shown us, and the sacraments constantly remind us, and our liturgy provides us the brave space to know, that in our pain there is healing, in our wounds there is transformation, and in death there is new life.

If re-engaging our chaos does not allow us to sit with others' chaos or engage deeply with the chaos of the world, with injustice, with suffering, with the "groaning of all creation" in its becoming, then we are not really engaging. Addiction/sin is an invitation to our own depths and our individual potentialities and possibilities, and at the same time with the depths and possibilities of everyone around us. Engaging with our individual depth leads directly to our ability to be in touch with everyone's individual depth and in turn the depth that undergirds all of creation. "As the sponge-like body of the creation is thus encompassed, so also it is penetrated. By the same principle each finite body is thus surrounded and permeated by infinity[;] . . . these beginning-waters of creation flow again as birth waters, in which even a dying body may find grace."[8]

8. Keller, *Face of the Deep*, 82.

8

The Jesus Movement

The other blessing in my year away from school was the setting within which I worked. It was a small outreach mission in downtown Tallahassee whose congregation was made up almost entirely of those who were unhoused or living at or below the poverty line. We served ten meals a week and had two Sunday morning Eucharists and a Tuesday night evening prayer and healing service. I started there two days after I arrived in Tallahassee, feeling utterly broken, helpless, and beyond repair. I was given the gift that year of living and working with a community of people who shared their lives with me in vulnerability and openness, and through that community I found healing.

Everyone I was with on a daily basis was struggling in some way. Many people in the community identified with some specific addiction, often drugs or alcohol. Many people were without a home or very close to being without one. Many people lived and slept on the street, while others were in low-income housing or stayed at the nearby homeless shelter. Either way, I was able every day to arrive at the mission feeling broken, vulnerable, and beyond hope and to be in community and relationship with people who felt the same way. I have no idea what it is like to be without a home. I am privileged through my race, sexuality, socioeconomic status, and education, and thus I cannot compare my experience directly to that of anyone who was there. What I did learn was that homelessness is not a circumstance reserved for people who have some sort of limitation. It could happen to anyone. It helped me realize that anyone and everyone is one bad day away from this kind of physical vulnerability. The community of that mission helped me be human in a new way.

It only happened because we were a community of people who had no choice but to gather and share the ways we were suffering. There were no facades to put up, there were not material possessions to hide behind, there was no way to hide the suffering that was being felt in the community—and through that openness to suffering I felt healed. Little by little, one interaction at a time, I was able to speak out my suffering, lift up the source of my pain, and without judgment let it be held by this beloved community of mutual suffering.

This is where I learned that the foundation of Christianity, the thing at the very heart of its theology and tradition, is not rituals, confessions of doctrine, or belief in one theory or another about Jesus. The heart of Christianity, the cornerstone on which it is built, is healing. Christianity is first and foremost a tradition of healing, and I felt that tradition every day in that community. It came not through confessions of faith, but through confessions of pain. It came not through belief in doctrine, but belief in the lifelong journey of suffering and transformation. It came not through unflinching faith, but open-ended uncertainty.

There is healing power in the Christian tradition, a healing power that I first felt through the communal gathering of people open to their own suffering and the suffering around them. I found healing in community, but only after everything had fallen apart. Only after I had let all my beliefs and theories die. Only when I had come back, face to face, with others, and let them witness to my suffering and was allowed to bear witness to theirs.

The Mission of the Church

Within the Christian tradition there is an area of theology called missiology, focused on the church's mission in the world. For most of the church's history, mission was focused almost exclusively on conversion. In a movement away from the colonial undertones of such missiology, today there is an increasing emphasis not on conversion but on discerning what the mission of God is in the world and how the church is called to take part in that mission. Thus, the question becomes one of humility, rather than certainty on the part of the church, driven by discerning the ways God is moving in the world rather than the concrete assumption that mission is about creating more Christians. For some, this conversion model may still be the focus, but in a twenty-first-century context, with addiction, sin, and healing as central concepts in the salvific mission revealed through Jesus, we are called to something new.

As we transition to the next stage in the history of Christendom, many people in Western mainline churches are feeling the squeeze of knowing that the direction and structure of the church must change while still not having full clarity on what that direction and structure should look like. There are always more answers: we need more millennials, we need more young families, we need to care more about liturgy, we need to abandon Sunday morning altogether, we need more music, we need less music, we need more social gatherings, we need less social gatherings. The list goes on and on. The problem, though, is not in needing to find new answers, the problem is in needing to find a new question.

For decades leading up to the twenty-first century, and now almost two decades in, the church has been asking itself, "How do we get people to come back to the church? How do we make the church relevant in people's lives? How do we compete with all those other options out there that are taking up people's precious time?" All these questions seem to be based on the same underlying assumption: we need to be something new that we as of yet have not been. The problem is not that the church hasn't yet found the answers to the questions, the problem is that the questions we are asking are flawed. They are based on a false assumption that we do not yet have what we need to be relevant and that we do not yet know how to be of importance in people's lives.

Instead of doing something new, what if the church did something old, ancient even? The institutional church of the twenty-first century is being called in humility to occupy the little patch of ground that it was created to inhabit. This is not to try to be as fun as a movie or a concert, or as relevant as a pop star or a celebrity, or as exciting as a sporting event, or as fancy as a country club, or as intellectually adept as an institution of higher education. Instead, standing barefoot on the soft earth that is its unique place in the world, the church can be a window of God's grace in the world. It can be a communion of people, a gathering of the sad, tired, sick, friendless, unfun, lonely, boring, needy, frustrating, annoying, and hurting, who recognize their sinfulness and share it openly. The church was made to be a place of vulnerability, relationship, healing, and peace. The way to do that is very simple, but is a very difficult calling indeed.

The Church of the (Twenty-)First Century

The church of the twenty-first century has an important role to play in response to addiction. One part of that is to offer a theological framework for addiction and create a place for it in our understanding of the nature of God and of our own humanity. Another is to be a resource for the kind of healing for which the world around us is yearning. Both of these involve examining our cultural assumptions about addiction and then creating space in our theology within which addiction can be understood. It also presents a call to the church to look more like the church of the first century. As a member of the church of the twenty-first century I can't help but see the disconnect between the where the church is now and where it is being called by the suffering in the world around it, and by the suffering of those within it. There are several trends in Western culture today that point to the fact that the church is being called to radically shift its focus and structure, and to recall its original intention, which it finds in the Gospel witness to the life and ministry of Jesus, including his death and resurrection.

One such trend is the general decline in people claiming any kind of religious identity. There are growing demographics of people commonly referred to as "nones" or "spiritual-but-not-religious." Often, the lens through which the institutional church has understood this phenomenon is to try to figure out new ways to market old ways of doing things in order to draw people who fit into these categories back into the church or to the church for the first time. The assumption that underlies this kind of behavior is that it is our job to communicate to people who claim little or no affiliation to the church why we are still relevant to their lives.

One of the problems with this approach is that it is a one-way mode of communicating. It assumes a kind of spiritual colonialism, where the church is claiming to have all the answers for someone else's spiritual and religious life and it is just a matter of finding the right combination of words to change their mind about it. The church is trapped in this way of thinking. What this phenomenon is calling us to do is engage is some deeper self-reflection about what we have become in the eyes of the world. For someone to say that they are spiritual but not religious, and therefore not part of any religious institution, may be telling us that, in their eyes, the church has become a religious institution disconnected from the spiritual needs of the world around it. It is not that our grandest traditions and liturgies are being overlooked in terms of their importance in people's lives, but that we have lost sight of the vital spiritual truths inherent in our Christian tradition and how they connect to our lived experiences.

Many churches still live and die on Sunday morning liturgies and average attendance. We are no longer in the manipulative power position to dictate to the culture our own position of prominence. Rather, the church now finds itself in the humbling position of listening to the yearning of the world and then responding. For many members of churches, it is hard to describe to non-churched or de-churched people why Christianity is important, because much of institutionalized Christianity has become disconnected from human experience and suffering. It is the church's job now to rediscover the power of its own teaching for spiritual transformation and healing. Jesus did not plant churches and ask people to worship him. Jesus communed with suffering people and loved them, dived deep into the human experience, and modeled the healing power of dying and trusting God to bring us back from the dead. The Christian narrative has vital spiritual importance to the world, but we have to experience it before we can communicate it, and if we in the church are disconnected from its place in our own lives and from our own suffering then we will never be able to do that.

The Jesus Movement

If we are going to take seriously the journey, not just the death, of Jesus as a roadmap for our spiritual path we must look at the way Jesus built and interacted with community. In the recent life of the Christian tradition, there has been an emphasis on being the "Jesus movement" present in the world today. Since his installation as Presiding Bishop of the Episcopal Church in November of 2015, Bishop Michael Curry has been speaking about his vision for the church at a time of persistent inner turmoil and anxiety about falling membership numbers and dying churches. Bishop Curry has made a call to the church, saying boldly, "This is a moment for the church to reclaim its share in the Jesus movement."[1] This is Bishop Curry's way of calling the church back to its roots. It is his understanding that "Jesus came to start a movement,"[2] and therefore it is time for the church to locate itself back in that original movement which Jesus started.

The most basic understanding of the Jesus movement can be constructed from what we know of the life, ministry, and community of Jesus

1. "The Jesus Movement—Presiding Bishop Michael Curry."
2. "The Jesus Movement—Presiding Bishop Michael Curry."

of Nazareth. The Jesus movement is most basically understood as the movement within first-century Judaism that Jesus led through preaching, teaching, and gathering. Bishop Curry emphasizes that the "Jesus movement is about evangelism, about forming followers, disciples of Jesus, and it is about making witness through personal service and public prophesy."[3] While these are all clear aspects of Jesus' ministry, there was something even more foundational to Jesus' movement in the first century to which we must return.

In his award winning text, *Christianity: The First Three Thousand Years,* Diarmaid MacCulloch asserts that, "Christianity had no specific ethnic or social base, and to begin with it was a movement too insignificant to leave artefacts or even much trace in literary sources outside those which Christians themselves created."[4] His conclusion, therefore, is that uncovering the aspects of this earliest movement of Christianity brought about by Jesus is only possible through documents created by the earliest Christians, chiefly the Bible. Therefore, to really get a sense of what the Jesus movement was during Jesus ministry we must look at it through the texts that we have in the New Testament.

In the Gospels, more than anything else, what is most foundational to Jesus' ministry is gathering people and sitting with them, though he does not gather and sit with just any people. The Jesus movement was about Jesus gathering together and sitting with sinners, the broken hearted, the sick, the poor, the needy, the destitute, and the downtrodden. Jesus' life was spent speaking and being with the people on the margins of society, who had been cast away and forgotten. As Jesus makes clear in Luke's Gospel, "Those who are well have no need of a physician, but those who are sick; I have come to call not the righteous but sinners to repentance." As MacCulloch asserts, Jesus' teachings were "a chorus of love directed to the loveless or unlovable, of painful honesty expressing itself with embarrassing directness, of joyful rejection of any counsel suggesting careful self-regard or prudence."[5] At its most basic, Jesus' movement was about gathering together sinners, who were in touch with the pain of their sins, and bringing about transformation and healing to those who seemed beyond God's love.

At the same time, the Jesus movement is not about Jesus sitting with people out of pity for their pain, but in solidarity *with* their pain, knowing

---

3. "The Jesus Movement—Presiding Bishop Michael Curry."

4. MacCulloch, *A History of Christianity*, 112.

5. MacCulloch, *A History of Christianity*, 88.

they are all dealing with the pain of missing the mark. Reclaiming our part in the Jesus movement is not about *ministering* to the unloved and unlovable, but sitting down and recognizing that we are one of them, and they are one of us. The Jesus movement is about the recognition that we are all sinners, all missing the mark, and that Jesus is sitting there with us. It is, as illustrated in the Gospel account, people gathering together, in honesty and vulnerability, and recognizing the ways they are missing the mark, in the promise of transformation and healing.

Bishop Michael Curry's call is for us to reclaim our place in this movement of gathering, of communal recognition of what is not working, and of transformation and healing. To say that we need to reclaim our place in this Jesus movement is to assert two things. One is that we have lost our place in it or given it up. The other is that it is still going on and we need to find our place in it once again. Therefore, we must recognize that the Jesus movement as we believe it was in the first century of early Christianity, is still going on today. It's even going on in our churches, but it is happening in the basements and classrooms and spare rooms of our churches instead of in the sanctuaries. It is happening when a group of people gathers together in mutual recognition that they are missing the mark in their daily lives and behaviors. It happens when these people gather together and admit that they are powerless over these powerful ways of missing the mark and proclaim that only a power greater than them can heal them, transform them, and bring them back to sanity. The practices at the core of the Jesus movement are happening today, and we know them as twelve-step groups.

The Movement among Us

The church is playing host to a recovery movement that is promising the very transformation and healing that we as Christians are called to promise, and we can use this model to reclaim our place by going back to the very essential truths on which Jesus built his movement. I am not saying that the church should coopt or absorb the twelve steps, that we should ban them from our churches or resent them for the effective work they are doing. Much to the contrary, we can examine what is happening in the church today and let the twelve-step movement inform how we reclaim our place in the Jesus movement, while also reclaiming dimensions of our own tradition as tools on the road to our recovery and that of others.

For instance, defines addiction as "a disease," a "problem of brain chemistry," and "a physical, mental, and emotional illness that yields most surely to a *spiritual* remedy."[6] They go on to suggest how we respond to addiction in congregations, suggesting that parishes "make space available in your buildings for recovery groups to meet," "schedule recovery events such as talks in your education program by recovering people," and schedule a once-a-year "Recovery Sunday," which is a "celebration of the deliverance by God's grace of persons who have been imprisoned by a punishing and bewildering illness."[7]

While the emphasis on having recovery ministries is vastly important in order to begin conversations about this difficult issue, there is another step to take on the journey. We need to move past a disease model of addiction, we need to move past talking about addicts as the *other*, and we need to recognize our own contributions to healing rather than relying solely on twelve-step programs. We, as church, have a stake in this game, and instead of resenting twelve-step programs, instead of not talking about addictions and letting someone else handle it, I propose we work side by side and recognize that we as a church have something unique to bring to the recovery process.

The teachings of Jesus, the acts of Jesus, and the life, death, and resurrection of Jesus are all about transformation and healing of sins. Sin and addiction are one and the same processes of aiming for something transcendent and eternal, missing the mark, and then feeling the suffering of that attempt. What we see in our churches is two groups of people, one in the sanctuary and one in the basement, seeking recovery from *the same spiritual process*. The church, as evidenced in Jesus' life and ministry, is meant to be a group of people who recognize all the ways they are missing the mark, and coming together, not because it is a social standard, not because it is part of a Sunday morning routine, but because transformation is happening in the gathering.

The Eleventh Tradition of Alcoholics Anonymous states, "our public policy is based on attraction rather than promotion; we need always maintain personal anonymity at the level of press, radio, and film."[8] In other words, people show up to twelve-step meetings because they work. They come because someone who was transformed by working the steps shared

6. Recovery Ministries of the Episcopal Church, "Read All about It."
7. Recovery Ministries of the Episcopal Church, "Read All about It."
8. *Twelve Steps and Twelve Traditions*, 96.

with them their story of recovery and spiritual awakening and they said, "I want that too." The Eleventh Tradition says that this movement will not grow because it is well promoted or because it has the best tag lines or most relevant programming. It will grow because people will be transformed through it, and that message will be something that cannot be kept quiet.

What We Have to Learn

To reclaim our place in the Jesus movement is to recognize that the church will grow when it is a place of transformation and healing, not when it has the best advertising or most appealing websites. Instead of looking for people to get in the doors out of fear of decline, let's be intentional about our place in the Jesus movement and trust that we are in fact a place of transformation. We will never be the modern branch of the authentic Jesus movement without talking about addiction and sin. To view addiction as an invitation to something deep within ourselves is to recognize not only that it is at its core a spiritual process, but also that it is a means for transformation and healing. In the same way, we recognize sin as an invitation to transformation and growth. This means that we can begin to approach addiction and sin not as evil things that foster shame and need to be swept under the rug, or immoral action that must be hushed. Instead, Jesus models for us the openness that we need in order to talk about our pain and suffering as it pertains to the ways we sin in our lives. This is the openness modeled in twelve-step meetings.

Working a program of recovery involves working the steps, working them with a sponsor and regularly attending meetings. In these meetings, people take uninterrupted time to share with the group how they are doing in their recovery work. These meetings last about an hour, where everyone is given time to share the blessings and trials of their day or week, and then people are given the opportunity to take a chip if that meeting is marking the beginning of a new recovery process for them. When the meeting is over, people are free to talk and spend time together outside the parameters of the formal meeting. While not everything needs to be about how painful life is or how much we are missing the mark, this is where it needs to start.

This, of course, is a fundamental truth of Jesus' ministry and teaching. The twelve-step groups show us a model of people coming together to talk openly about their addictions, about the painful ways they are missing the mark. By approaching addiction and sin in this way, without judging them good or bad, right or wrong, we create the space to share our experiences of sin and addiction openly. Viewing addiction as an invitation releases us from deciding what is right and what is wrong. It releases us from judging who is and isn't "saved." It releases us from deciding who is and isn't hurting or needs to be healed or needs to recover and helps us realize that we are all in need of recovery. If we see people coming together in a similar Jesus movement around a common desire for healing, transformation, and awakening, why are we not more curious to learn from this movement and then reclaim our place in it?

We, as the church, are a community built on the idea that we are all sinners, that we all need to recover and that there is something about our human experience that keeps us separated from the transcendent, yet deeply connected to it and yearning for it. We share the common belief that Jesus can bring transformation and healing into our lives. So why are we still talking about ministering to addicts and not sitting together recognizing that we are all addicts or, to say it in another way, that we are all sinners? We are all human and all missing the mark in some way, and that is in itself a grace of God. Addiction and sin are filled with grace because they wake us up to what is not working, to what is "not God" in our lives, so that we can repent, which in the Greek literally means to "change our minds." It is then that we can turn back toward God's grace and have God move through these sins and addictions to cultivate in us life from death, to cultivate healing and transformation from the deepest wounds, and to cultivate wholeness from brokenness.

The Power of Community

As a community founded on the life and teaching of Jesus, we are built for transformation, we are built to recognize God's grace, we are built to be a place for healing and recovery, but we are missing one crucial step. We are missing the first step. We are not talking openly about our sins. The first of the twelve steps is "We admitted we were powerless . . . that our lives had become unmanageable."[9] If we, as Christians, cannot sincerely sit down together and say that we are powerless to not "miss the mark" in our lives, in full humility and truth, then we have completely missed the good news of Jesus Christ. We have become passive observers of the Jesus movement that we all desperately want and need to be a part of.

9. *Twelve Steps and Twelve Traditions*, 21.

So what are we to do now that we can see addiction and sin through this spiritual grace-filled lens? We can be the church, but first we have to clean the lens through which we view addiction and sin, and by doing this begin to recognize that talking about them is not an admittance that we are bad or evil, but that we are human. In recognizing that these very human behaviors are in fact manifestations of deep spiritual yearnings, we can recognize not only our humanity, but our co-occurring divinity. Taken together we get a glimpse at the most primary implication of the incarnation, which is that we share in both Jesus' humanity and divinity. We are all inextricably linked to God, and yet we are unquestionably human, and both are a blessing beyond words.

We are called to an open-ended interactivity, where our addictions are invitations to this inter-relationality where we are all only able to grow and heal when we are in relationship with one another. When we "other" someone, when we welcome the addict without recognizing our own addictions and accepting their invitation, we are shutting ourselves off to this interactivity. It is only when we can find ourselves all on the same level, where there is no first or last, in the egalitarianism of the kingdom of God, that we can be in authentic relationship and share ways in which we are suffering with one another. In sharing and hearing these stories we grow in this dynamic interactivity of relationship. Truth of God, self, suffering, and healing is relational. It can only be born in the unfolding of relationship. We build trust in community, and thus reveal truth. We build trust by trusting and pledging our truth to one another in relationship. We do not overlay truth onto relationship, but allow relationship to reveal truth to us: the truth of ourselves, the truth of one another, and the truth of God.

When we can come back together, face to face, and let ourselves recognize that these othering barriers are illusory, we can share, vulnerably, as equals, as siblings, as children of God, what is hurting in our lives. When we share and hear we break down the barriers that restrict the movement of the Holy Spirit in our lives. It is then that the Spirit of God can hover over the face of the deep again, create from the chaos of our lives, and bring us into the truth of who we are being called to become.

We cannot do this work by ourselves. We cannot walk this path removed from community. In the story of the bronze serpent from chapter six, the sources of suffering were only transformed into sources of healing when lifted up before the entire community of the Israelites. It was both an individual healing and a communal witnessing to suffering. In our journey of lifting up and gazing at our sources of suffering, we require not just our own gaze, but the gaze of a community to bring about this transformation. This is the power in naming suffering, admitting powerlessness, and claiming our addiction in community, where we can be heard and seen and gazed at by other people. It is through the return of this gaze, being seen for who we are in all vulnerability and powerlessness, that we are healed and can become sources of healing for others. This is what it means to lift up our serpents onto our staff, to take up our cross and be hoisted up onto it. We are laid bare before the gaze of all, and through that gaze we both die and are resurrected, and raised to new life.

In community we can let our ideas of God be cracked open and bring us to new and uncertain depths together. It is in our depths that we can recognize that the impossible is possible, that addiction is itself a grace and suffering is healing, that the bad is the good and the infinite is the finite, and that death is the path to life and sin the path to freedom. It is in our inner depth, our communal depth, and the depth of God that we bear witness to the reality that truth is evolving, that we are being transformed, and thus taking part in the great unfolding of the universe where things once never fathomed to have been true are revealed to be eternal.

Conclusion

Where Do We Go from Here?

Since my time in Tallahassee, I have tried to continue in my intentionality of reflection and practice. I have continued to do contemplative prayer and to try every day to hold gently my own chaos and that of the world. I have not mastered this practice. To the contrary, I fail at it regularly, but I find that I often grow more in the practices I fail than the ones in which I convince myself I have triumphed. When I first encountered contemplative prayer and began a daily practice of it I believed that it was going to lead me on a straight path to inner peace and quiet. I thought that if I did it right and did it long enough, over the course of some number of years I would leave suffering, fear, anxiety, and chaos behind.

I have learned in the years since that this is not the case. It is comforting to believe that such a practice has a goal and a measurable outcome. In practicing contemplative prayer I have not left behind suffering, anxiety, fear, or chaos. These things are just as present as ever in my life, if not more so. What has happened is that the practice has cultivated within me the ability to sit with them, let them be, and let them teach me.

If anything I have said is true, if anything I have said resonates with you, it is only by the grace of God. It seems that the more I write, the more I learn, the more I read, the less I know and the less certain I am of anything. I am less certain about the assertions made in this book now than when I started writing it. I understand why Thomas Aquinas, after finishing his long work of theology, wrote that it was all a bunch of straw. It is all a bunch of straw. Everything that has been said and ever will be said about God, about us, about spirituality, about addiction, about transformation, all pales in comparison to what is actually true. It is all but a shadow of its reality. As Paul said, we see in a mirror darkly. And so I have set out to put in words something that is wordless, that is beyond description, but the truth of which is communicated only through relationship, through sharing stories, and through the honest struggle to communicate what I believe to be true about myself, about God, and about addiction.

I have not escaped addiction, but through practices of engagement I can see it, engage with it, and let it lead me to something more. I still want to look at pornography. When I am alone, tired, sad, or frustrated I still have that compulsion to open the web browser and lose myself in videos and images. Right now, as I type this on my laptop, I am keenly aware that pornography is a click, type, and search away. It is still at my fingertips. It is still inside and will be forever. But something about it has changed. It feels like, every time I speak about it, write about it, or hold it up in the light of day to be seen, it changes shape and transforms. It does not shrivel and die, it does not get taken out by the root. It becomes slowly transformed into a guide to my depths. While it still feels like these depths are infinite, I also can't help but feel that I can befriend them and descend them lovingly with God.

Opening and Responding

Theology is often described as systematic, but not because its aim is to be able to explain everything without leaving any room for mystery. Theology is systematic in the same way that an eco-system is, in that the way you understand one thing affects the way you understand everything. In the interconnectedness of an ecosystem, if one part of the system is affected it leads to every part of the system being affected. So it is with theology, in that the way we understand one part of our theology affects how we understand every part. To make a claim about God is to make a claim about everything else as well. To make a claim about humanity is to make a claim about the entire theological ecosystem of thought and belief. When we claim that we have a fallen, sinful, corrupt humanity we make a claim not just about humanity, but God, creation, salvation, and everything else that takes part in that system.

It is because of this truth that we must examine all of our theological assumptions and closely explore each and every word we use when talking about ourselves, one another, and God. When we use the language of disease to describe addiction we are taking on assumptions about ourselves and others that have significant implications for how we understand every part of the world around us. If we think that some parts of ourselves are good and some bad, then we can believe that there are some good parts of creation and some bad parts. We can believe that there are some good people and some bad people. But if every one of us is created in the image of God and all of creation was molded by the hand of God, where is there room for deviation and evil? Instead, we are invited through addiction to reimagine our understanding of the suffering in our lives and in the lives of the world and to witness God's grace at work. In all its pain and sorrow, addiction is somehow a grace of God, always calling us back to engagement with our depths and to befriend the chaos and suffering in and around us.

Jesus' words from the Sermon on the Mount call to us today as loudly and clearly as they ever did. "Then he began to speak, and taught them, saying: Blessed are the poor in spirit, for theirs is the kingdom of heaven. Blessed are those who mourn, for they will be comforted. Blessed are the meek, for they will inherit the earth" (Matt 5:2–5). Somehow, in this world of striving, superiority, and egocentricity, we are called to be poor in spirit. We are called to mourn. We are called to be meek. Too often we find ourselves trying to climb the ladder, and yet we hear Jesus over and over again asking us to climb further and further *down*. This is our work. This is our lifelong spiritual journey. This is the path that Jesus has asked us to follow him on. Yet, this is so counter to our instinct to outperform, out-earn, and outlast the world around us that we often miss it completely.

We are living in a world that is increasingly aware of its addictions. We are addicted to drugs and alcohol, we are addicted to gambling and sex, we are addicted to the internet and smartphones, we are addicted to victory and superiority. And yet Jesus preached a gospel that shows that victory is in defeat, and superiority is in inferiority. Power is in powerlessness, richness is in poverty, and comfort is in mourning. We live in a world of deep yearning, deep pain, deep suffering, and even deeper transformation. We preach a gospel that says that healing is found in woundedness and soothing is found in pain.

In many ways, though, we have become disconnected from the very pain that leads to soothing and the suffering that leads to transformation. It is thus our work, as a community, as a church, and as a people of faith to reclaim our place in this holy journey of death and resurrection. Addiction is not an evil that needs to be swept under the rug and silenced, but an invitation from God to walk this journey toward spiritual wholeness. Addiction is an outward and spiritual sign of a deep inward and spiritual yearning for the eternal, the transcendent, and the divine. We are invited to see sin and addiction as parallel spiritual processes, following the same path of yearning and missing the mark.

Based on this parallel process of sin and addiction, the church as a community can draw from the wisdom of the twelve steps of AA created by Bill Wilson in order to inform a complementary response to addiction. Addiction and twelve-step recovery can positively influence how we approach sin in our community. This approach is based on an understanding that the sacraments are constant reminders on our lifelong journey of the truth that death leads to transformation and new life. The deepest purpose of the sacraments is to bring us to ever-greater depth, humility, meekness, poverty in spirit, and union with God.

We are here, in a world racked with pain and suffering, as a people constantly aware of the pain and suffering in our own lives. What we can do, when we understand addiction as a spiritual process, is begin to look at what those behaviors are in our lives that are causing us pain, why we are engaging in them over and over, and then come with humility to share with others who are travelling on this same journey. We are *all* missing the mark somehow. We are *all* addicted to something. What we can do as a community is be gentle with ourselves and gentle with those around us when it comes to issues of addiction. When we view addiction as an invitation to spiritual wholeness, we see that, even in its pain, it is a blessing and a possibility. God's grace is always moving in our lives, and addiction is no exception. It is time for us to start recognizing this in ourselves and in others, to treat others with the understanding of this truth, and to walk this path together, openly, honestly, and gently.

There are so many things around us that we believe will make us happy. These things are not evil in themselves; they just are not the time-less, eternal experience of God for which we most deeply long. They do not usher us into the "peace of God which surpasses all understanding" (Phil 4:7) or the "Sabbath-rest" that still "remains" for us (Heb 4:9). Only when we become aware of how we are missing the mark, hurting ourselves and doing it all in the name of an ever-allusive happiness, will we, as Julian of Norwich says, "see it." Only then will we realize just how fleeting all of the noise, movement, and happiness are that the world can give. Only then will we be able to rest in the unflinching simplicity and depth of God, in which we all take part.

There are many kinds of sound, but only one silence. There are many kinds of movement, but only one stillness. There are many kinds of happiness, but only one peace. It is a peace that is not conflict avoided but conflict engaged, a stillness in action, a wound that is healing itself, a death that is life, an engagement with suffering that is not about removal but about transformation. This is the depth to which we are invited, and it is in addiction that we find the invitation. The only question is, are we willing to open it and respond?

Bibliography

Anonymous. *Alcoholics Anonymous*. 4th ed. New York: Alcoholics Anonymous World Services, Inc., 2001.

Augustine. *Four Anti-Pelagian Writings*. Translated by John A. Mourant and William J. Collinge. Fathers of the Church Patristic Series Vol. 86. Washington, DC: Catholic University of America Press, 1992.

Brown, Brené. "Why Your Critics Aren't the Ones Who Count." YouTube, Dec 4, 2013. Online: https://www.youtube.com/watch?v=8-JXOnFOXQk

Catholic Church United States Conference of Catholic Bishops. *United States Catholic Catechism for Adults*. Vol. No. 5–450. Washington, DC: United States Conference of Catholic Bishops, 2006.

The Cloud of Unknowing: With the Book of Privy Counsel. Translated by Carmen Acevedo Butcher. Boston: Shambhala, 2009.

Episcopal Church. *The Book of Common Prayer and Administration of the Sacraments and Other Rites and Ceremonies of the Church: Together with the Psalter or Psalms of David according to the use of the Episcopal Church*. New York: Church Hymnal Corp., 1979.

Fitzgerald, Robert, Ed Dowling, and Bill Willson. *The Soul of Sponsorship: The Friendship of Father Ed Dowling, S.J. and Bill Wilson in Letters*. Center City, MN: Hazelden-Pittman Archives Press, 1995.

Frazier, Jessica. "Natural Theology in Eastern Religions." In *The Oxford Handbook of Natural Theology*, edited by Fraser N. Watts, John Hedley Brooke, and Russell Re Manning, 166–81. Oxford: Oxford University Press, 2013.

Jellinek, E. M. *The Disease Concept of Alcoholism*. New Haven, CT: Hillhouse, 1960.

"The Jesus Movement—Presiding Bishop Michael Curry." Video. Anonymous, 2015.

Johnson, Robert A. *Owning Your Own Shadow: Understanding the Dark Side of the Psyche*. San Francisco: HarperSanFrancisco, 1991.

Julian of Norwich. *Showings*. [Revelations of Divine Love.] Translated and introduced by Edmund Colledge and James Walsh. New York: Paulist, 1978.

Keating, Thomas. *The Human Condition: Contemplation and Transformation*. New York: Paulist, 1999.

Keller, Catherine. *Cloud of the Impossible: Negative Theology and Planetary Entanglement*. New York: Columbia University Press, 2015.

———. *Face of the Deep: A Theology of Becoming*. London: Routledge, 2003.

———. *On the Mystery: Discerning Divinity in Process*. Minneapolis, MN: Fortress, 2008.

BIBLIOGRAPHY

Kurtz, Ernest. *Not-God: A History of Alcoholics Anonymous.* Center City, MN: Hazelden Educational Services, 1979.

MacCulloch, Diarmaid. *A History of Christianity: The First Three Thousand Years.* London: Allen Lane, 2009.

May, Gerald G. *Addiction and Grace.* 1st ed. San Francisco: Harper & Row, 1988.

Nakken, Craig. *The Addictive Personality: Understanding Compulsion in Our Lives.* San Francisco: Harper & Row, 1988.

National Institute on Drug Abuse. "Drug Abuse and Addiction." 2015. www.drugabuse.gov.

Palmer, Parker J. *A Hidden Wholeness: The Journey toward an Undivided Life.* San Francisco: Jossey-Bass, 2004.

Recovery Ministries of the Episcopal Church. "Read All about It." https://episcopalrecovery.org/message.

Rohr, Richard, and Russ Hudson. *Laughing and Weeping: The Enneagram as a Tool for Our Spiritual Journey.* Edited by Richard Rohr and Russ Hudson. Compact Disc. Albuquerque, NM: Center for Action and Contemplation, 2009.

Teresa of Avila. *The Way of Perfection.* [Camino de perfección.] Translated by E. Allison Peers. Mineola, NY: Dover, 1946.

Tillich, Paul. *Dynamics of Faith.* New York: Harper, 1957.

Twelve Steps and Twelve Traditions. New York: Alcoholics Anonymous, 1953.

Williams, Rowan. *Being Christian: Baptism, Bible, Eucharist, Prayer.* Grand Rapids: Eerdmans, 2014.